LOVE FOR IMPERFECT THINGS

'A wonderful book . . . Zen teacher Haemin Sunim describes
with great clarity the suffocating effect of perfectionism – how
damaging it is to think your worth as a person is solely
dependent on how you perform. Then, page by page,
he shows you how to reclaim your freedom and your life'
Mark Williams, co-author of *Mindfulness:
Finding Peace in a Frantic World*

'The world could surely use a little more love, a little more
compassion and a little more wisdom. In *Love for Imperfect Things*,
Haemin Sunim shows us how to cultivate all three, and to find
beauty in the most imperfect of things – including
your very own self' Susan Cain, author of *Quiet*

'Heartwarming, calming and simple . . . filled with wisdom and
powerful truths that will teach us to love ourselves first in order
to transform our relationships with our loved ones'
Hector Garcia, author of *Ikigai: The Japanese
Secret to a Long and Happy Life*

'Haemin writes beautifully and simply so these vital life-
lessons resonate easily and deeply' Miranda Hart

HAEMIN SUNIM

TRANSLATED BY
Deborah Smith and Haemin Sunim

ARTWORK BY
Lisk Feng

PENGUIN LIFE

AN IMPRINT OF

PENGUIN BOOKS

LOVE FOR IMPERFECT THINGS

How to Accept Yourself in a World Striving for Perfection

PENGUIN LIFE

UK | USA | Canada | Ireland | Australia
India | New Zealand | South Africa

Penguin Life is part of the Penguin Random House group of companies
whose addresses can be found at global.penguinrandomhouse.com.

First published in Korea by Suo Books 2016
This translation first published in the United States of America by Penguin Books 2018
First published in Great Britain by Penguin Life 2019
001

Published with the support of the Literature Translation Institute of Korea (LTI Korea)

Printed in Italy by L.E.G.O. S.p.A.

A CIP catalogue record for this book is available from the British Library

ISBN: 978-0-241-33112-5

www.greenpenguin.co.uk

CONTENTS

LOVE FOR
IMPERFECT THINGS

True freedom is being without anxiety about imperfection.

—Sixth-century Zen master Sengchan

PROLOGUE

THERE ARE TIMES IN LIFE when we encounter a film that stays with us for a very long time. For me, *A River Runs Through It* is one such film. Set in the first half of the twentieth century, and with the beautiful scenery of Montana for a backdrop, it tells the story of the Maclean family, for whom fishing is just as important as religion. The father is a Presbyterian minister with two sons. The elder son, Norman, lives a respectable life and becomes a university professor. The younger son, Paul, comes to lead a life of debauchery while working as a journalist for a local paper; his gambling habit gets him into great debt, and in the end he is beaten to death in an alley. The father, consumed by his deep sense of loss, speaks to his congregation during Sunday service with restrained emotion, revealing his love for his second son. "We can love completely," he says, "even without complete understanding."

It was difficult for the father to understand why his son Paul had to live a life of dissipation. However, this didn't stop him from loving his son—because, to him, love transcends human understanding. Rather than loving someone only when you feel you understand what it is you love, the kind of deep, enduring love shown by the father does not cease even when the loved one behaves in a way you do not agree with. In the depths of the heart, love is always flowing, like a river.

WHEN WE EXAMINE OUR LIVES, we see many imperfect things, like motes of dust on an old mirror. There are all kinds of things that leave us feeling dissatisfied and unhappy: Our words are often different from our actions, our relationships are strained by our mistakes, our best-laid plans for the future go awry. On top of that, in the course of our lives we inflict various wounds on others, intentionally or unintentionally, causing us to feel guilt and regret.

But it's the same when we look at our family and friends. The child who doesn't listen to what his parents tell him; your own parents who do not understand you; your spouse who doesn't behave reasonably. Close friends with bad health habits make you worry about their well-being. Every morning when we watch the news unfold, we see that the world is filled with yet more fighting, more accidents, more discord. It seems as though it will never end.

And yet, even though we find many such imperfect things in the world we live in, we cannot help but love them. Because our lives are far too precious to be spent in ridicule and hatred of what doesn't appeal to us, of what we do not understand. As we become spiritually mature, we naturally develop more empathy and try to see things from others' perspectives. This, in turn, teaches us to accept the imperfections of others, and of ourselves, in a more graceful and compassionate way, like a mother loves her child no matter what.

I have collected here my reflections on learning to look at the world and myself more compassionately. I have been inspired by people who have shared with me their life stories and questions during my public talks or on social media; they have opened my heart and deepened my wisdom. I pray that this book can be a friendly hand for you in a moment of despair, and bring you peace in a time of difficulty.

—HAEMIN SUNIM
The School of Broken Hearts, Seoul

Chapter One

SELF-CARE

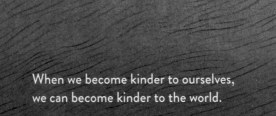

When we become kinder to ourselves,
we can become kinder to the world.

DON'T BE TOO GOOD

WERE YOU ONE OF THOSE CHILDREN who were praised for being "good"? Did you then try hard to be good by always agreeing with parents, teachers, or older relatives? Even if sometimes it was hard, you learned not to complain and bore it quietly? And now that you're an adult, do you still feel a responsibility to please other people? Do you constantly make an effort not to disturb or be a burden on others? But when there's someone who makes things difficult for you, you try just to ignore it or put up with it, because it is not in your nature to do or say something that can potentially hurt someone or make someone feel uncomfortable?

I HAVE MET MANY GOOD people who suffer from depression, panic attacks, and other emotional disorders due to difficult human relationships. Such people tend to be gentle, well mannered, and solicitous of others. They are the kind of self-sacrificing person who will habitually put other people's wishes before their own. Why, I wondered, do such good people often fall victim to mental and emotional suffering?

I, too, was introverted and meek as a child, and so was often praised for being "good." A good son who wouldn't give his parents any trouble, a good student who listened to his teachers—all this taught me was that it was good to be good. But when I went to graduate school, I began to feel that there might be a problem with only being good. In group work with students who were smarter than I was, with stronger personalities, I found that the tasks everyone wanted to avoid somehow always fell to me. I kept on telling myself that it was good to do good, but as time went by it started causing me quite a bit of stress. When I opened my heart and spoke honestly to an older friend who was in the same program, he gave me the following advice:

"Be good to yourself first, then to others."

It was like being struck by lightning. Up until then, I had only ever worried about what other people thought of me. I had never once thought properly about caring for myself, or loving myself.

When we say that someone is "good," we often mean that the person complies with the will of others and isn't self-assertive. In other words, people who are good at suppressing their own desires in deference to another's are the ones who frequently get called "good." If someone always listens to me and follows my advice, naturally I like that person and think of him or her as a good person. It seems that "good" sometimes refers to a person who thinks too much of others to be able to express his or her own will.

While it is not always the case, there is a particular pattern that can be seen in our relationship with whoever raised us as a child. Many who are self-effacing in this way grew up with a dominant father or strong-willed mother. Or as a middle sibling, who received relatively little attention from the parents, giving rise to a strong desire to win the parents' recognition by obeying them in all things. In certain cases, when the parents' own relationship is not good, or the family dynamic is awkward in some way, there are also those who take it upon themselves to make their parents happy by being "good."

But the problem is that, by living in accordance with the demands of others, we unwittingly neglect our own desires and needs. If as a child you were indifferent to your own feelings, minimizing them or not considering them important, as an adult you will not be able to tell what it is you yourself want to do, or who you are as a person. And then when you encounter someone who treats you unfairly or makes things difficult for you, since you do not know how to properly express your own feelings, the anger that ought to be directed toward its instigator is trapped inside you and ends up attacking you instead. "Why am I such an idiot, that I can't express my feelings properly, can't even speak up honestly?"

ABOVE ALL, PLEASE REMEMBER THIS: What you are feeling is not something that should just be ignored, but something very significant. The feelings inside you will not easily disappear just because you decide to suppress or ignore them. Many psychological problems come about when repression becomes a habit and the energy of those suppressed emotions is unable to find a healthy outlet. Just as stagnant water becomes fetid and toxic, so it is with our emotions.

But it's not too late. From now on, before going along with what others wish you to do, please listen to the voice inside you, telling you what you truly want. Even when you feel yourself buffeted by constant demands, if you really do not want to do something, don't try to push through with it, exhausting yourself to the point that you are no longer able to cope. Instead, try to make others understand what you are feeling by expressing it in words. Don't worry that expressing yourself will cause the other person to dislike you and the relationship to become strained. If the other person knew how you really felt, she probably wouldn't have made such demands of you.

Even when everyone says, "Let's all have coffee," if you want a chai latte, it's okay to speak up and say, "I'd like a chai latte instead." We consider it good to be good to others, but don't forget that you have a responsibility to be good to yourself first.

✳

Learn to express what you are feeling
without agonizing over it.
It is a life skill every bit as important as
learning how to read. Without it,
dissatisfaction builds up, arguments break out,
and relationships can blow up like volcanoes.

✳

Does it make you feel frustrated
to be the only one doing the work?
If so, don't just swallow the feeling; speak up:
"It's difficult for me to do it on my own.
Could you please help me out?"
Little by little, expressing your feelings
will become easier.

✳

When someone asks for a favor,
don't forget that you have the option to say,
"I'm terribly sorry, but I can't do that."
You have no obligation to take on a task
that will be a great burden on you.
And if the relationship grows strained
because you do not do the favor,
it was never a good relationship to begin with.

*

Just as on a plane,
you are told to put
the emergency breathing mask on a child
only after you have put one on yourself,
there is nothing selfish about looking after yourself first.
Only if you are happy will you be able
to make those around you happy.

*

When you care for yourself first,
the world will also find you worthy of care.

*

In the same way that when you're in love and
you want to spend time with only that person,
try spending time on yourself—
you deserve your care and attention.
Treat yourself to a delicious meal,
a good book, a nice walk with a lovely view.
As you would invest in the person you love,
so you should invest in yourself.

＊

My dear friend:
Because there is some part of you
that is imperfect or broken,
it can motivate you to work hard
to overcome it, and can ultimately
bring you success in life.
It can also help you relate to others
and become more compassionate.
Do not despair over what is imperfect in yourself.
Instead, look at your flaws with love.

＊

It's okay that you have flaws.
How could our lives be as clean and white
as a blank sheet of paper?
Life naturally takes a toll
on our bodies, our minds, and our relationships.
Rather than choosing a life in which you do nothing
for fear of making a mistake,
choose a life that improves through failure and pain.
And shout out loud to your struggling self,
"I love you so much."

*

In our hearts we all carry secrets
that we cannot easily share with others.
They can be about illness, money,
sexuality, relationships, or family.
They can evoke a deep sense of
inferiority, shame, anxiety, or guilt.
But because of the weight of the secrets,
we become more humble and understanding.
Don't judge people based on how they appear,
as they may have difficulties that nobody can see.

*

Seeing on social media how your friends are
enjoying themselves,
have you ever felt envious?
One of our common mistakes is
to compare how we feel inside
with how our friends appear outside.
We don't know what is going on inside of our friends,
but we are well aware of what is going on
inside of ourselves.
Your friends might be envying you based on
your social media posts,
without knowing what is really going on in your life.

＊

Have you ever felt a sense of inferiority
because of a cousin who is doing better than you?
She may be smarter than you, attend a better school,
work at a better company. But remember that
none of us can know how our lives
will turn out in the end.
Though school and work might be measures of success,
the older you get, the less important they will be.
The true winner is the one who is happy with his life.

＊

You may appear unattractive
not because you have many unattractive qualities
but because you think you do and look so uncomfortable.
Even if you have unattractive qualities,
if you are confident and at ease with yourself,
you won't have such a problem.
Remember that the most attractive quality
is your confidence.

✻

It's okay not to be ranked
first, second, or even third.
Compare yourself not with others,
but with the old you.
Like yourself for making an honest effort.
And continue to have faith in yourself.

✻

If you keep letting criticism upset you,
then you will gradually wither,
and in the end you will not be able to do anything.
And that is exactly what your critics are hoping for.
Do not let those who criticize you determine your destiny.
Every time you hear from your critics, shout more loudly:
"No matter what you say, I won't give up.
Let's see who is right in the end."

✻

"Why should your life be destroyed
by the easy criticism of those
who do not know you or care about you?"
—SEOK-CHEON HONG,
KOREA'S FIRST OPENLY GAY CELEBRITY

＊

If you begin to believe what others say about you,
they will begin to control you.
Not everything that appears in your mind is true.
Do not let someone else's opinion rule your life.

＊

"If you hear a voice within you say,
'You cannot paint,'
then by all means paint,
and that voice will be silenced."
—Vincent van Gogh

＊

We are worthy of being loved
not because of what we do well
but because we are precious living beings.
Even if you don't achieve
the perfection the world demands,
your existence already has value
and is worthy of love.

✳

In India, "Namaste" is a common greeting, like "Hello."
But there is a beautiful meaning to "Namaste."
It means, "The divine being within me
bows to the divine being within you."
We are much greater and more sacred than we think.

Don't think you are lovable only
when you succeed at what the world demands.
You are already worthy of love.

YOUR EXISTENCE IS ALREADY ENOUGH

To MY DELIGHT, SEVERAL GROUPS of Buddhists from New Zealand and Australia invited me to come and give a dharma talk. So for the first time in my life, I got to cross the equator and flew to Auckland and Sydney. Even though it was a long way from Seoul, I was looking forward to this trip because it would also give me a chance to visit my closest graduate school friend, who'd studied with me in the United States. He'd moved back to Australia after receiving his Ph.D. and had become a professor. It had been over a decade since I'd promised to visit him. Each time I saw his Christmas card, which arrived without fail as each year drew to a close, I would recall the promise that I'd so far failed to keep. Now that the opportunity had come about, I was really looking forward to seeing him again.

On the other side of the equator, the weather was the opposite of what it had been in Korea. The temperature on the day of my talk was over ninety degrees Fahrenheit. And I learned that in the Southern Hemisphere, if you want a house that gets a lot of sun you have to choose one that faces north. Also, rivers tend to flow north rather than south, and in the night sky the Southern Cross takes the Big Dipper's place. Though they were literally the polar opposite of the place where I had been living, New Zealand and Australia didn't seem as foreign as I might've expected, especially their people. Well aware of the lonely and busy lives in modern cities, I was honored to be able to offer them some words of comfort and wisdom.

WHEN THE VARIOUS TALKS WERE OVER, I headed to my friend's house. I rang the bell, and he opened the door and greeted me with a big smile on his face. We reached to clasp each other's hand and embraced, like family members long separated by the Korean War. Though ten years had gone by, he looked very much the same, aside from his hair having thinned slightly and his body having filled out a bit. He was as outgoing and warmhearted as ever, and as I also knew his wife, Jane, from our grad school days, I felt at ease in their company.

After dinner, we drank tea on the terrace as the sun went down, and laughed out loud at how we were already middle-aged. Our hearts were still those of students; we could not believe we had become men over forty. As old friends, we were unguarded and revealed our inner feelings freely. Old friends have no need to display artificial selves; you can accept them as they are and share your true self with them. He was such a friend for me. He told me everything that had happened over the past decade, talking until he reached his recent worries.

I remembered that he had always been anxious, even with nothing in particular to be anxious about. He told me that his anxiety had gotten worse recently, and to stave it off, he had been working hard. Jane was concerned that his health would suffer if he continued this way. He worked every night at his computer, even after midnight; he rarely got a good night's sleep; and he was always busy. Of course, his hard work had earned him recognition in the academic world, and a swift promotion at his university, but not only could he not stop working, he also was overcome with anxiety when he had no work to do.

Night had fallen, and it was chilly outside. We went inside to avoid the mosquitoes and sat on the sofa. My friend put on some quiet music and poured himself a glass of wine. He told me that he'd had a tough childhood. In the eyes of the world, his father had achieved success, but he took out his work stress on his family. His father would transform into a different person and become violent when he had been drinking. He even beat my friend. So my friend felt like he was walking on thin ice at home. When his father was in that state, his mother would leave the house to avoid him, and in her absence my friend had to look after his younger siblings, pretending for their sake that it was all a game. That was when he became increasingly nervous, never knowing when his father might drink and explode.

Reflecting on how it had been for my friend when he was young, I made a guess as to where his anxiety and workaholism came from. Wanting to help him however I could, I spoke carefully. "Because each person's situation is different, it's difficult to draw any firm conclusions, but one of the known causes of becoming a workaholic is growing up feeling unworthy of your parents' attention unless you do something great, as opposed to feeling loved and cared for unconditionally. This also tends to be the case with children of successful parents who are too busy with their lives and show little interest in their children's lives. To win their parents' attention, such children feel under constant pressure to do things to please their parents. Otherwise they feel unlovable, and their actions are devoid of meaning. In your case, it makes sense that you have developed this constant feeling of anxiety, given your father's violence when drinking. It must have been very difficult for you with your mother not there to protect you. Never knowing when your father might explode, you probably thought that the only way to prevent it would be to do everything he wanted you to, and to do it correctly. Now, as an adult, your father is gone. However, it's the world's demands rather than your father's that are making you feel anxious—that if you don't do everything that's asked of you, and do it correctly, your existence has no meaning or worth."

My friend nodded, seeming to agree with what I'd said.

"But the truth is, you are already worthy of being loved. You don't need to be convinced of your self-worth by taking on society's demands and living up to its expectations. You already are a precious being and deserve to be loved and cared for. Look inside and see if you can find the child within you, still shaking with anxiety because of his father. Send the energy of loving-kindness to that inner child, and look at him compassionately. How difficult it must have been, coping with your father's rage alone, trying to protect your siblings, without even your mother to help you."

At this point, both my friend and I were in tears. My friend closed his eyes for a while, then said calmly: "You're right. There is still a little kid inside me, trembling with anxiety, unable to be loved. And he is pleading with me not to ignore him anymore. All this time, I made myself too busy worrying about the opinions of others while suppressing the inner wound from the past. I need to believe that I am worthy of love for who I am."

As I WAS LEAVING HIS HOME a few days later, I left a brief note for my friend:

When we were in graduate school, you were like a big brother to me. You helped me overcome several crises. You don't know how grateful I am even now, when I think of your kind heart. And so for goodness' sake please remember: Even if you never achieve anything big and significant, to me, your existence alone is already enough.

＊

Don't let your difficult past
define who you are today.
If you do, you will live your whole life
as a victim of the past.
There is life force within you
waiting to shoot out of the ground of the past.
Please trust that force of renewal.
Bow respectfully to your past and proclaim,
"From now on, I have decided to be a little happier!"

＊

If someone is unable to think beyond himself,
it could be because he didn't get enough love growing up.
Because he felt that the world was cold and uncaring,
he had to be self-centered to take care of himself.
If there is a selfish person in your life
who makes things difficult for you,
look deeply into his pain
and try to understand where he is coming from.

*

If we examine what motivates us,
we see that even as adults
we want recognition from other people,
and that so much of what we do
comes from that desire to be recognized.
Shower your child with attention,
and make her feel secure in your love.
This way she won't grow up starved for
other people's acknowledgment.

*

If one of your children is jealous of
her brother or sister,
take her on a trip, however brief,
just the two of you.
If a trip is impossible, spend a whole day
only with her.
Eat something delicious together,
play in a park, and listen to her.
If children do not receive enough attention,
psychological problems often emerge.
Parents can prevent this while their children are
still young and impressionable.

*

Every now and then, permit yourself a little luxury.
Whether it's buying beautiful flowers for the dinner table,
a slice of delicious cheesecake to have with a caffè americano,
a pair of soft winter gloves—
little luxuries can brighten your life.

*

The nice cutlery set, tea, wine, clothes, pen, quilt
that you have been saving for a special occasion—
use them whenever you get the chance.
Special moments are not separate from our everyday lives.
When you make use of something special,
it makes the moment special.

*

Do you sometimes feel that
something small can bring you a lot of happiness?
I feel that way when I see
yellow and orange peppers.
I often hesitate to buy them, since they are
more expensive than green peppers.
But I love their colors,
and when I do decide to treat myself,
they make me so happy.
And did you know that bell peppers have
three times as much vitamin C as oranges?

*

If I like myself, it is easy for me to like people around me.
But if I am unhappy with myself,
it is easy to feel unhappy with those around me.
May you become your own biggest fan!

*

When I extend a small kindness to others,
I find it easier to like myself.
If you feel that your self-esteem is low,
try doing something nice for a stranger.
As you begin to like yourself,
your self-esteem will improve.

*

Even products labeled "limited edition"
are made on a production line with hundreds that are exactly
the same.

But there is only one you in the world.
Please cherish the unique individual that is you.

*

The head says,
"Do not hate that person too much,"
"Forgive others for your own sake,"
"Do not envy your friend's success."
But there are times when the heart does not listen.
At times like these, give prayer a try.
Prayer connects the path between head and heart.
Ask humbly for help with what seems to be impossible
at the moment.

*

People sometimes express their longing
through hate.
If you hate someone,
look closely within yourself.
What could the reason be?
Are you still attached to that person?
There is no opportunity as good as this
to be mindful of ourselves.
We send rockets all the way to the moon,
but when it comes to our own mind,
the closest thing to us,
we remain utterly unaware and ignorant.

*

Though we should not ignore
what other people say,
the decision is ultimately ours to make.
When you make a decision,
listen to your heart more than the opinions of others.
A decision made because of the opinions of others
is one we often come to regret.

✳

There is a saying in Korea:
"Lengthy deliberation often leads to a terrible decision."
If you think and worry too much before doing something,
"your boat goes to the mountain instead of the ocean."
Now and then it is necessary to trust your intuition
and push ahead in the direction you feel is appropriate.

✳

When you have an important decision to make
and are not sure what to do,
stop for a while
and listen to what your heart is saying.
Take a walk in a park
or a brief trip somewhere beautiful,
or meet a friend you can trust
and discuss what you have been thinking.
Your heart is far wiser than your head—
it already knows the answer.

＊

When your head thinks "yes" is the right answer,
and yet something doesn't seem quite right,
take a little more time,
and do not give the final answer just yet.
There are times when intuition hits the mark
and rational thought doesn't.
If you allow yourself a little time to discover
why you are hesitating,
the reason will soon become clear.

＊

Everybody needs time alone.
When you've spent the whole day at work
being harassed by others, and then return home
to find your family won't leave you in peace,
you can easily become annoyed and angry.
At such times, do not blame yourself for getting annoyed.
Instead, take some time for yourself by stopping by
your favorite bookstore, coffee shop, or temple.
Go for a quiet walk alone and listen to your favorite songs.
Being alone makes the world pause for a moment
and helps to restore harmony.

＊

Just as a mother looks at her child with love,
look at your own suffering with compassion.
You will soon feel that you are not alone.
There is a soft inner core of love and caring
at the heart of every suffering.
You are not thrown into this world alone.

Chapter Two

FAMILY

It can feel like a mystery
why my child, parent, or sibling is
thinking and behaving a certain way.
But although we may neither
comprehend nor like it,
we can nevertheless love them,
because love transcends understanding.

"PLEASE LOOK AFTER MOM"

EVERY PERSON IN THIS WORLD is someone's precious child, and a Buddhist monk is no exception. Even though monks have left home and become ordained in pursuit of spiritual enlightenment, most do not cut ties with their parents. Maudgalyayana, one of the closest disciple monks of Sakyamuni Buddha, was famous for his filial love for his mother. According to Buddhist scriptures, he descended to hell in order to rescue her. Kyeongheo, the great Korean Zen master of the nineteenth century, also remained a good son to his mother after becoming a monk. Upon having an experience of enlightenment, the first thing he did was to search for his mother. Kyeongheo lived with her and spent nearly twenty years looking after her. Following Kyeongheo's example, many monks nowadays are taking care of their elderly parents in one way or another.

In my case, too, each time I return to Korea, I try to stay with my parents for at least a week, hoping to make up for my absence. But whenever I do, I feel sad to see how much older they have become, especially my mother. Many gray hairs have sprouted on her head, and many teeth have fallen from her mouth. She is not as active as she used to be. It is distressing for a son to see his own mother becoming old. Although I know that everything in this world is impermanent, I cannot help but wish that my mother might be exempt. I am a lot like my mother. She is an introvert, but with a bright and warm personality. She loves music and art and enjoys reading books, just like I do. If she hears or thinks of something insightful or interesting, she likes to write it down and share it with her family and friends. She can be patient and strong in the face of difficulties. She is also proud of my writings and talks, as they have helped many people.

But a while ago I found out that my mother, whom I had assumed would always be healthy and well, had become ill. It seemed she had kept her illness from me because she didn't want me to worry about her. Nothing makes your heart sink more than when you get a phone call from your father telling you that your mother is sick. I dropped everything and flew to see her. Though luckily her illness was treatable, I stayed with her for a full month. It made my heart burn with shame to think that while I had been busying myself trying to help strangers, I had been neglecting my own parents.

When I give a public talk, I usually close by inviting the audience to meditate together. First I guide people to offer love and good wishes to themselves while caressing their heart. Afterward I ask them to hold hands with those sitting next to them and to close their eyes. Then I ask them to imagine that they are holding the hand of someone they deeply love and care about, like their mother. Finally I ask them to send love to the people they just imagined and to repeat this blessing: "May you be happy! May you be healthy! May you be peaceful! May you always be protected!"

Chanting quietly together like that, a good number of people shed tears. Though we always wish our loved ones to be happy and healthy, we often do not express it, assuming that they already know how we feel. As we repeat the blessing, we regret that we have not spent enough time with our loved ones because we are too busy. I, too, felt that way as I was imagining holding my mother's hand while chanting the blessing along with the audience. As the words sank in, all of a sudden the following sentiment rose up from the abyss of my heart:

"Mom, Mom, I love you so, so much."

Without realizing it, the word "mom" came out instead of "mother." Though it was a little embarrassing, I texted that message to my mother right away. Thinking about it, I couldn't remember when I had last said these words to her. Later, I heard that receiving such an innocent message from her grown son, who had left home to become a monk, made my mother cry a great deal. And then she resolved to become healthy again, not just for herself but also for her son.

IN THE FAMOUS KOREAN NOVEL *Please Look After Mom*, the daughter realizes how much she loves her mother only after her mother goes missing. In an interview, the author, Kyung-sook Shin, said that she had been planning the book for a long time but couldn't get it quite right until she changed "mother" in the title to "mom." The novel ends with the daughter on a trip to Vatican City. The daughter lays a rosary in front of the *Pietà*—an image of the Holy Mother embracing the dead Jesus—and prays, "Please, please look after Mom."

After staying at home with my mother for a month, I had to leave the country again. My heart was filled with sadness and remorse, and again and again I found myself summoning the name of Avalokitesvara Bodhisattva, Mother of Mercy and Protection, for my own mother.

*

Something as simple as holding someone's hand
can go a long way toward easing that person's pain.
The more we hurt, the more we need
the love and support of our family.

*

When someone you love is in pain,
the most meaningful gift you can give is your kind presence.
Sending flowers and texting are good,
but not as good as sitting with her, holding her hand,
looking into her eyes, and giving her a kiss.

*

We live longer now not because we do not get sick,
but because we have learned to manage our illness.
To those who are fighting illness,
and those who are caring for them,
may you not lose hope!

✳

Even when the weather forecast calls for rain all day,
there are times when, if we look closely,
we see that the rain lets up.
Even though we are ill and in pain,
if we look closely, we see that
there are moments without any pain.
But if we say to ourselves,
"I am sick" or "It's going to rain all day,"
then we feel that the rain or pain never lets up.

✳

Sometimes we want to be told
"I need you" more than we do "I love you,"
because we want to feel
that our lives have a purpose.
So, be brave and say honestly, "I need you."

*

When a beloved family member passes away,
we feel sorry for not having looked after them better
and guilty for not having protected them from harm.
Then, after many difficult and lonely nights,
the spring, which we thought we'd never see again, returns.
As the warmth of the spring sunshine touches our face,
we feel as though the departed is still with us,
wishing us happiness.
We assumed we were alone
but then realized we were not.

*

Losing someone precious to us
is like losing the compass that pointed to life's meaning;
it seems as though we will never find true north again.
The experience of life's impermanence is a great lesson.
For those of you who are suffering, may this experience
become
an opportunity to wake up to the Truth beyond
impermanence.

*

No matter how good a relationship is,
it is inevitable that it will change over time.
A close friend may move to another city,
or a family member may pass away.
Your circumstances, too, can change.
But don't let this make you too sad—
because when one door closes,
another one always opens.

*

"Some people come into our lives and quickly go.
Some stay for a while and leave footprints on our hearts,
and we are never, ever the same."
—FLAVIA WEEDN

*

The greatest gift that parents can give their child
is to be happy themselves.
If the parents are happy,
then the child can grow up into a happy and confident adult.
But if the parents are not happy,
then the child can feel worthless—
unable to make his parents happy no matter what.

*

You sacrificed your life for the sake of your children.
But instead of being thankful, your children are angry
that they have been living their parents' dreams
rather than their own.
Look back and see if you deluded yourself into believing
that being obsessed with your children was a sacrifice.
And consider whether your "sacrifice"
did not rob your children
of the opportunity to learn for themselves.

*

There are many aspects of life that we cannot control.
When it comes to our children, spouse, relatives, and friends,
we can love them, pray for them, show them interest,
but we cannot control them,
even when we have good intentions,
since their happiness ultimately depends on themselves.
Let them take responsibility for their choices.
When we get through an illness, we develop immunity.
If we protect others from illness,
they may not develop proper immunity against life.

*

If a teacher coddles her students, she will spoil them.
It is the same with your children.
It is often the case that your younger children,
whom you paid less attention to,
grow up to be more caring toward their parents
than your eldest, whom you took such trouble over.

*

The reason adolescents don't listen to their parents
and stubbornly try to have their own way
is that they are learning to be independent.
It is normal, so don't worry too much.

＊

Children want to admire their parents.
You won't win their admiration by being overprotective.
Instead, offer your help to the weak and powerless,
or make an honest effort to model important values,
such as honesty, compassion, dedication, and tolerance.
Do your best to give your children someone to look up to.

＊

Parents, please teach your children that
abusive language or violence toward the weak
is wrong under any circumstances.
It is also wrong to delight in someone else's pain.
If you wish for your child to grow up to be decent,
do not countenance such behavior.

＊

In oppressive and violent relationships,
no one can take care of yourself but you.
If a relationship causes you pain,
then draw a firm line and distance yourself
from the other person.
Once you are apart, you will hear your internal voice
and gradually become stronger and more independent.
Do not lose your grip on the reins of your own life
and allow yourself to be dragged around by someone else.

＊

In the course of giving advice,
I often hear from young people who are conflicted
because they love their parents but also hate them.
There is nothing wrong with having these two emotions.
You can love and hate someone at the same time.

＊

It is nearly impossible for a son or daughter
to change a parent's personality, values, or behavior.
Even if children consider their parents
problematic in some way,
they have neither the right nor the responsibility
to change them.

*

If you were often rejected or ignored
by your parents while growing up,
you can end up seeking the love and attention
you were denied from your romantic partner instead.
If your partner is even slightly indifferent toward you,
then the wound from your childhood can be ripped open,
causing a big fight with your partner.
But the real cause isn't your partner;
it's the wound you are carrying within you.
Rather than projecting this wound onto your partner
and causing a fight,
set aside your pride and speak from the heart:
"I am terrified that you will reject me and leave me,
like my mom did."
If we combine painful memories, the need for attention,
and pride, the relationship can easily be ruined.

*

If you assume that, since you've been together for so long,
you should be able to read each other's minds,
there are so many things you will fail to understand about
each other.

I love you.
I thank you.
And I need you.

UNDERSTANDING OUR FATHERS

I WAS ANGRY AT MY FATHER. "Father, why did you keep putting off going to the hospital? I told you many times not to do that." Despite myself, I was irritated and worried. And I disliked speaking to my father this way. Here's what had happened. When I had finished my autumn retreat at Bongam Zen Monastery and gone to visit my parents, I saw that my father had become quite emaciated. I asked if there was a particular reason he had lost weight, and he said there was no particular reason, it was just his digestion acting up, so he'd been taking some medicine now and then. Hearing this, I was suddenly worried that it might be stomach cancer, since the first symptom of stomach cancer is weight loss for no apparent reason. And hadn't my grandfather passed away from stomach cancer?

But despite my advice, my father refused to have a gastroscopic examination. Insisting that he was fine, he asked me to look after my own health instead. "I'm not important, but you, my son, do so much good for people, you have to look after yourself properly so you can keep on helping them." When I returned home that bone-numbingly cold winter, my father had been suffering from a cold and rhinitis for over a month. This time even he admitted that he felt there was something strange going on inside him, and he agreed to the gastroscopy. My heart sank. Why don't you value your own body? Why do you constantly say you're not important? Why don't you think of your children, of how much you're making them worry? I was upset.

IT SEEMS I'M NOT THE ONLY one to experience such emotions. I've noticed that people tend to experience more difficult and complicated emotions in their relationships with their fathers than with their mothers. This seems especially to be the case with sons. And so, based on my conversations with people, I came up with five prototypes of father-child relationships— although there are certainly many more. As you read them, see if any of the five match your case.

The first case is one in which the father behaves in an excessively patriarchal way, withholding affection and strictly enforcing rules and standards. He often controls his children by making them feel shame and guilt. To his children, such a father looms large, like a mountain that cannot be crossed. Even as adults, his children do not feel comfortable around him, having spent their childhood afraid of him, and cannot bring themselves to open up and have an honest conversation with him.

The second case concerns children who have witnessed the suffering of their mother because of their father's extramarital affairs or lack of employment. Such children tend to develop deep sympathy for their mother and rage toward their father. If, as children, they were unable to express their anger toward their father, their repressed emotions make it difficult for them to engage with their father as adults. They often choose to avoid their father altogether.

The third case is when the father is a self-made man, a firm believer in the power of hard work who has similarly high expectations of his children. Given that the father had to pull himself up by his bootstraps, it's not enough in his eyes for his children to work only moderately hard, to do only fairly well in school. Desperate for their father's approval, as adults they are often plagued with anxiety and unable to relax, because they feel they are worthy of love only when they do something well or achieve some great success. I frequently meet young people who have an excellent education and a good job yet have low self-esteem and workaholic tendencies; speaking with them, I discover that many of them have had this kind of father.

The fourth case concerns children who are born into ordinary families and who turn out to be academic geniuses or to otherwise have great success. Such children feel somewhat constrained by their father, and resent him for interfering in their lives. They are independent and self-motivated and prefer not to receive unsolicited advice from a father who can't really know what their lives are like. Such children love their father but do not necessarily look up to him.

Finally, the fifth case is children who lost their father when they were young. While growing up, they felt their father's absence profoundly; as adults, they still long for him. They tend to remember their father as a hero and are attracted to teachers or mentors who are like him in some way.

I WANTED TO UNDERSTAND why my father constantly said he was not important, and so did not value his own health. As I do when talking with a stranger, I made an effort to understand him deeply. It was the first time I'd ever tried to see my father not in relation to me, as my father, but as a man. And what I saw was a boy whose own father, my grandfather, had rarely shown him any affection or expressed interest in him. My father was still pained by the memory of my grandfather going away to seek refuge during the Korean War, and taking only his eldest son with him. My father, the second son, was left behind with his mother and sisters. Rare delicacies, like a fried egg, were always reserved for the eldest son. Plus, as men tended to be in those days, my grandfather was brusque and patriarchal and didn't show much emotion. Having grown up in the shadow of his father and elder brother, my father was unable to see how precious his own existence was. Even now, old enough to be a grandfather, he lacked confidence and thought of himself as unimportant, after a lifetime of having to put other people first. All of a sudden, I felt my eyes grow hot.

AFTER THE GASTROSCOPY WAS OVER, my father called and told me that he was in luck: It wasn't stomach cancer. He hesitated, then said, "I love you, son." It was the first time he'd ever said those words to me. Instantly, heat flooded my chest. Knowing that my father will read this, I want to say to him: "Dad, I love you, too. And I am truly grateful to you for raising a son with such high self-esteem and a positive outlook. I feel lucky that you are my dad."

Love needs no reason
other than love itself.

✳

When your self-esteem hits rock bottom,
say to yourself: "To my family and close friends,
I'm just as precious as I've always been.
I'm still capable of doing good in the world;
a few people who don't really know me
don't get to decide what I'm worth.
In time, I believe I'll meet different people
who will value me and my abilities."

✳

If you love someone,
rather than doing what you think they need,
do what they themselves ask you to do.
Though it comes from a good place,
doing what you think someone needs
can be the seed of wanting to control them,
to make them a certain way to please yourself.

＊

With a little planning,
you can continue to enjoy your life
while looking after someone close to you.
Sacrificing yourself completely
won't be good in the long run,
not even for the person you're taking care of.
Only if you yourself are reasonably well
will you be able to look after someone properly.

＊

Are you worried because
your spouse or child has put on weight?
The best way to make someone you love
look after their health is by looking after your own,
with a balanced diet and regular exercise.
If you set an example, they're much more likely to join in.

＊

Even though you did your best,
their response was lukewarm,
or they demanded even more of you.
There's no need to despair.
If you really did all you could, leave it be.
If they need more, they'll be able to find a way
to finish the job themselves.

＊

We sometimes resort to verbal threats
in the hope of making people come to their senses.
For example: If you don't do what I want,
I will take away something that is important to you,
or in the future I won't give you what you need.
This happens especially between family members.
Unfortunately, such words won't change people's minds.
They will only hurt them
and make them dig in their heels.
Instead, calmly explain why something is important to you,
so your words don't sound like threats or ultimatums.
Change will last longer when it's not forced
but when it comes about because
they have been convinced of its need.

＊

Someone told me this, and it made a positive impression:
"Haemin Sunim, now that I am doing so well financially,
my relationship with my siblings and parents has improved."
If you have made a lot of money, share some of it with your
family.

＊

Much domestic strife comes from
the futile effort to interfere and sow discord:
the wife, between her husband and his parents;
the mother-in-law, between her son and his wife;
the husband's sister, between her brother and his wife.

＊

However close a relationship is,
some questions are better left unasked:
"Why don't you lose weight?"
"Why aren't you married yet?"
"Why did you get divorced?"
"Why aren't you working?"
Please, keep these thoughts to yourself.

✳

"Even among branches that stem from the same root,
there will be those that are healthy and bear many fruits
and those that are stunted and whose fruit is undersized.
The healthier branch might have become that way
by receiving more than its fair share of nutrients.
It's the same with siblings:
If there is one who is smart and successful,
there could be one who is poor and must rely on the other.
You'll be annoyed if every time your sibling asks for help,
you feel you're being deprived of what's rightfully yours.
But if you consider how your sibling
might have had to sacrifice
for you to get to where you are now,
it will not seem so unfair."
—MISOOK KO, KOREAN LITERATURE SCHOLAR

✳

We get the most annoyed by
those who are closest to us.
And when the annoyance is on both sides,
an argument will inevitably break out.
When someone is showing his temper,
it could be because he wants us to hear
about his current situation and empathize.
Rather than arguing,
try to understand his deeper needs.

*

When you feel like you're about to lose your temper,
think of your family.
Think about how your children will suffer the consequences.
If you cannot control your temper for yourself,
control it for your family's sake.

*

If a child is crying or making a racket on a plane,
you'll likely get annoyed with the child and resent the parents.
Imagine the child is actually
your niece or nephew, your grandson or granddaughter.
If we think of the child as a stranger,
we focus on the inconvenience to ourselves,
but if we think of the child as a family member,
we become merciful, wondering whether the child
is uncomfortable or in pain.

*

If you want to help your child, your partner, or your friend,
simply listen without offering advice
or your own interpretation.
And empathize, imagining that you yourself
just had that experience.
Don't turn away from difficulties, but endure them together.
That is how you can be of greatest help.

＊

Before you lay your head on your pillow and go to sleep,
recall just three things you were thankful for today.
If you continue to do this for two months,
you will see an increase in your level of happiness,
because instead of focusing on what is wrong with your life,
you will develop a habit of looking for what is good.
A happy mind-set needs practice.

＊

If you give something your full attention,
whatever it is, and examine it closely,
it will come to attract your interest and care.
Just as the face of your child is the most familiar
and the loveliest thing in the world,
constant attention will turn an ordinary object
into an extraordinary one.

＊

If you take home a cat and care for it,
even one that's been abandoned and is dirty,
it won't be long before it becomes
the cutest cat in the world.

Chapter Three

EMPATHY

If you love someone:
Embrace him,
like the Holy Mother embraces Her
    one and only Son.
Listen attentively,
like there is no one else but him
    in the whole universe.
Look into his eyes,
like a soul trying to communicate
    after losing language.
Dance together,
like tomorrow is your final day
    on earth.

THE POWER OF HUGS

MAYBE YOU'VE HEARD it said that each time someone embraces you warmly, your life is extended by one more day? Of course there is no way of verifying whether this is actually the case, but none of us will have any trouble understanding the message. When we find that things are getting tough, a warm, wordless embrace can have more healing power than a logical, point-by-point explanation of why things are so difficult. Although I cannot get rid of your pain, I will still stand by your side and stick with you even during the most difficult times. The warmest way of expressing this is through a hug.

WHEN I FIRST CAME to the United States, it took a long time for me to get used to the Western way of greeting someone. Instead of bowing politely in the traditional Korean way, I had to learn the casual, unreserved way that friends greet each other—a quick nod and a "hi" when you pass each other on the street. I had to learn that a handshake is not just clasping the other's hand but also involves smiling, looking the other straight in the eye, and ensuring that your grip is not too strong and not too weak. But of all the various methods of greeting someone, the one that took me the longest to get used to was the hug. Especially since becoming a monk, I had become used to greeting people by *hapjang*—putting my palms together in front of my chest and bowing from the waist. Opening my arms wide and embracing someone made me feel somewhat shy and awkward.

But of course a greeting is not something that one does alone. If you are parting from someone and she opens her arms to hug you, holding out your hand for a handshake not only will make her flustered, but also suggests that you want to keep some distance, which could seem impolite. But after a while, once my relationship with a friend or colleague had become sufficiently close, I learned to hug. Mysteriously, the initial awkwardness has gradually disappeared, replaced with a sense of fellowship, intimacy, and warmth.

RECENTLY I HEARD about some interesting studies about hugs—scientific verification that they do indeed have health benefits. Anthony Grant, a professor of psychology at the University of Sydney, presented research results showing that, in addition to reducing anxiety and loneliness, hugs lower our levels of the hormone cortisol, which gets secreted as a response to stress; this, in turn, strengthens immunity to pathogens and lowers blood pressure. And according to Karen Grewen of the University of North Carolina at Chapel Hill, if a couple holds hands and hugs for twenty seconds before leaving the house in the morning, their stress index will be only half that of couples who do not do this. In other words, a brief, warm morning hug with someone we love provides us with a protective layer, insulating us from the stress of the day.

As a monk, there are times when I have to offer people such a protective layer. One such instance still lingers in my memory. It was at a book signing in a large bookstore in Seoul; I was signing one woman's book when she suddenly said in a choked voice:

"Haemin Sunim, two months ago my children's father passed away in a car accident. I've been in such a state of shock that I've barely been outside these past two months. My younger brother gave me your book as a present, probably because he felt sorry for me; I cried so much while reading it, right from the first chapter. For some reason I got the idea that if only I could meet you, that would give me the courage to go on, and to look after my two children properly. I live in the countryside, but I got the train early this morning to come up to meet you in person."

Her voice was shaking, and her face was streaked with tears. In that moment, without realizing what I was doing, I got up from my seat, moved toward her, and opened my arms. After embracing her warmly for a while, I said: "I, too, will pray for your children's departed father. His spirit will probably be watching you from the other world, seeing how you go on living, how well you look after the children. Right now you are terribly lonely, and life is very hard, but through this experience you will become stronger, wiser, and more compassionate. From now on, things will gradually get better. Don't worry too much."

I held her as she wept, and thought to myself: Though I am lacking in many ways, I want to be a person who can bring some small comfort to people, who can give them courage, like a ray of warm sunshine. If there is someone who needs a hug from me, I will do it willingly, gladly, and as often as they need. Those of you who are reading this, if you have family or friends who are going through a hard time, please remember to give them a warm hug now and then. Who knows, you really might extend their lives—and yours, too.

＊

Because I have experienced pain,
I am able to embrace the pain of others.
Because I have made mistakes,
I am able to forgive others their mistakes.
May my suffering become the seed of compassion.

＊

If you want to express love to family or friends,
really listen to them,
devoting your whole mind and heart to their words.
If you listen with great care and interest,
they will come to feel, "I am a precious being,"
and, "This is what it feels like to be loved."

＊

Apparently seeing a photo of someone you love
can actually alleviate your pain, like taking Tylenol.
And if you see a person helping someone,
it boosts the happiness hormone inside your body,
as if you are the one lending a helping hand.

*

When your loved one is suffering and needs you,
just be there with her pain and suffering.
Let her feel she is not alone.
If you offer cheerful platitudes
or look for a quick solution,
it might be because you
do not want to face her situation.
Consider whether you are looking only for glib words
to quickly put yourself at ease.

*

I bumped into a high school friend
for the first time in many years.
He told me that when he saw his wife and children
waiting for him at the train station, holding umbrellas,
it made him realize his purpose in life.
The really important things are so near at hand.
And yet it seems we forget them now and then.

*

There are those who love you for who you are,
and there are those who love you for what you do.
There is no change in the love
of those who love you for who you are,
even when you make a mistake or fail.
Such people are your true friends and family.

*

To family or friends who have experienced a setback,
say, "Even though you didn't succeed this time,
I am very proud of you. Under difficult circumstances,
you didn't give up. That, to me, is a success."

*

I wish you to be happy.
But do not wait for someone to make you happy.
Make the decision to be happy for yourself, and act on it.
Do not surrender to someone else the power to make you
happy.

*

When someone asks, "How are you feeling?"
if you are unsure how to answer, just say, "Pretty good!"
The moment you answer like that, you may actually start to
feel good.

＊

When someone says something when they are tired,
remember that it is their tiredness speaking.
It is wise to leave important conversations
for the next day, after a good night's sleep.
When someone is tired,
bring them a cup of herbal tea
and just leave them be.

＊

One expression of love
is simply to leave someone to their own devices.

＊

Words hold great power.
"You will get better starting today!"
"You are so talented. You will become an amazing writer!"
"Your music will touch the hearts of many people one day!"
The moment someone says such words to you,
a new field of possibility opens up for you.
Words can become the seed of reality.

＊

Even though what someone says may be true,
if it is spoken with hatred and disdain,
it will make you reluctant to agree with the person.
We communicate not just with words,
but also with the energy of our emotions.

＊

What words are said is important,
but how they are said is often more important.
We also communicate through our facial expressions and
body language,
through the volume and tone of our voice.

＊

Words that convey anger, violence, or sharp critique
appear to have more of an immediate effect
than those that convey gentleness or compassion.
But the use of negative means can come back
to haunt the speaker,
causing him regret for hurting others for his own purpose.

*

If you get angry, your anger creates an echo,
bouncing back at you without fail.
Your anger arouses anger in others,
who retaliate either immediately with the same intensity,
or indirectly over the course of many years
in the form of gossip and passive-aggressive mind games.
So the next time you get angry, keep in mind the costs.

*

The house is a mess,
but you don't have energy to tidy it up.
In that case, invite your friends to your home.
Suddenly, you will feel a surge of energy which
can get the whole house tidied in thirty minutes!

*

When you are invited to a friend's house for dinner,
ringing the bell five minutes after the appointed time
seems the best thing to do.
There are times when arriving a little bit late
can be a big help:
an extra five minutes for the final dinner preparations.

＊

I saw the movie *Intern* and learned
that a gentleman who carries a handkerchief
does so not only for himself
but also for anyone he meets who might need one.

＊

When we help other people,
rather than thinking, "I am helping them for their sake,"
think, "I am doing this because I enjoy helping people."
Even if the people you help end up
not returning the favor, you won't be so upset.

＊

At a time of need, you were helped.
Now that things are better,
you would like to return the favor.
Unfortunately the one who helped you
is no longer in this world.
In such cases, please help young people
whose situation is similar to what yours was.
This will likely please the person who is no longer with you.

*

When the eminent monk Beopjeong Sunim
visited New York,
we took him to a nice bookstore in Manhattan.
Beopjeong Sunim told me generously,
"Haemin Sunim, choose some books for yourself."
Rather than picking out one or two,
I thoughtlessly gathered up a pile of eight,
using the excuse that I needed them for my studies.
Seeing this, a senior monk signaled to me
that I should choose only one.
But while I was hastily trying to put the books back,
Beopjeong Sunim saw and said,
"To a student monk, books are like the bread we eat
or the air we breathe."
He bought all eight books for me and even inscribed them:

Haemin Sunim, study diligently for your Ph.D.
and spread great teachings to many people.
Beopjeong, Palms Together

I feel great indebtedness to and love for my elders.
I wish to be generous to the younger generation like they
were to me.
I miss Beopjeong Sunim, who has already left this world.

When we love someone,
the greatest gift we can give
is to be fully present for them.

LISTENING IS
AN ACT OF LOVE

THERE ARE TIMES IN OUR lives when a really difficult situation comes up and we want to talk about it with someone. At such times, what sort of person do you generally end up seeking out? A friend who is smarter and a better talker? Or just one who seems like they will be on your side and listen warmly to what you have to say? In my case, I generally go for the latter. Of course, talking with a friend who is more intelligent than I am can indeed be helpful, because they can home in on my problem objectively. But the more difficult the problem, the more likely I am to be left feeling a bit dissatisfied by coldly rational advice, however sensible. I probably long for someone warm and caring who will listen to my struggling heart in an empathetic way.

Something like that happened when I was teaching in Massachusetts. There were many times when teaching brought me great happiness and fulfillment. But there were also times when all I felt was, "I am not cut out to be a college professor!"

For one, there were the cultural differences: Unlike students in Asia, for example, some students openly contradicted their professors. I welcomed those challenges and still believe that students should be allowed and even encouraged to have opinions different from those of their professors, but I was not used to the direct manner in which they refuted me in class. Sometimes I encountered students who were not serious about learning and came to class unprepared. They were a small minority, but as an inexperienced junior professor I was quite distressed and even a little depressed about this. I hated myself for disliking difficult students, which made me feel very uncomfortable and guilty.

Whenever I felt this way, I would want to talk it over with one of my senior colleagues. But rather than reaching out to those colleagues known to be clearheaded and direct, I usually ended up turning to senior colleagues who were kindhearted and good listeners. If I think about why, I would say it's because there's more to being a good listener than simply listening. From someone's facial expressions, tone of voice, and body language, we come to feel cared for and acknowledged and understood. When someone would focus on me, letting me say what I wanted to say without cutting me off or changing the subject, my troubled heart would begin to open up, and I would share those bottled-up stories one by one without fear of being judged.

That was a huge weight off my chest, and probably what I needed more than sound advice. After being a sympathetic witness to my situation, if my colleague were to share something similar that had happened to him, it would be an additional comfort knowing that I was not alone. As I started to have greater perspective, I found it easier to accept my situation and to deal with my feelings.

Being both a monk and a professor, I often have to give a public lecture or Buddhist dharma talk. But while certain audiences laugh out loud at my silly humor and leave the lecture hall looking pleased and enlightened, others sit blank-faced in heavy silence. Even when I give exactly the same talk, the overall experience is hugely different without a lively audience. If my audience and I are attuned to each other, my words flow like a river, coursing through the hall in an atmosphere of spiritual vitality. But if my audience is not very receptive, I shrivel psychologically and cannot get across effectively what I have prepared. This is why I believe that listening is not a passive activity at all. Listening openly, patiently, and attentively is one of the most significant expressions of love.

I sometimes wonder why we stay up late uploading photos and messages to Facebook, Twitter, Instagram, etc. No one forces us to; it's simply that we want to share with the world what we did that day, what we thought about, what photos we took. I think this has to do with the fact that we want someone to listen to what we have to say, even if that someone is the impersonal online world. Because only then do we feel that our actions have meaning, that our existence has value. Without people to pay attention to us, our lives would feel empty, like being alone on a stage without an audience. With this in mind, I would encourage people to think every once in a while about whether there are friends or family members going through a difficult time. Even though we may not have solutions to the problems they are facing, they will be grateful just to know we are willing to listen.

I think the process of healing begins when we open
our hearts and listen empathetically.
We can help people not because
we know the solutions to their problems,
but because we care enough to stay and lend our ears.
Knowing that others have gone through similar difficulties,
they become better equipped to cope with theirs.

＊

When we tell someone about our problems,
more often than not we do not want to hear
the "right words" from them.
We simply want to be heard.
When someone speaks to you,
do not rush to give them advice;
hear them out.

＊

Rather than trying to improve someone,
just be a mirror, reflecting them without judgment.
If you want them to improve,
you stop seeing them as they are.
Instead, you see only their shortcomings,
measured against your own subjective standards.

＊

Genuine love seems to love "in spite of."
Of course it is easy to love the parts we agree with,
but when we learn to embrace the parts we disagree with,
that is when liking turns into loving.

*

Children are eager to show off their scars
because they like to receive loving attention from others.
But if you look closely, adults are just the same.
When you are hurt or struggling,
when you are sad or depressed,
don't always keep it to yourself;
at times, bare your wounds like a child
and say, "I am in pain."

*

When we think we already know someone,
we stop making an effort to know them better.
When we do not know someone,
we make an effort to get to know them.
Love is the state of not knowing,
and of wanting to know more.
Consider whether you think you already know
your loved ones.
If you do, you are failing to see them as they are right now
and seeing them instead through the prism
of previously held opinions.

*

When you hear a close friend being slandered,
do you absolutely need to tell that friend?
If it will serve only to hurt your friend,
what is the point of sharing it?

*

The friend who backbites others in front of you
will probably backbite you when you are not there.

*

If you point out someone's faults,
don't expect their behavior to change.
Often all that happens
is that they get hurt.
Instead, praise their strengths,
which will grow to overshadow their weaknesses.

*

When you meet someone, compliment them,
even if it's just out of politeness.
Tell them they look happier, or healthier, or
that their outfit or hair looks especially good.
If you do, things will start off on the right foot,
and everything from that point will flow more easily.

*

In winter, going about Manhattan
in a gray quilted monk's robe,
I would sometimes hear people say:
"How original! Where can I buy one?"

*

Winter can be really cold, right?
I saw an advertisement saying,
"People are like heaters."
Our presence can warm each other.
May you be a heater for someone today.

*

Many of us experience disconnection
and related feelings like rejection,
disappointment, and loneliness.
If you are suffering in this way,
pray for the one who has broken away from you.
Send them some positive energy and good wishes.
Choosing not to hate them is the best revenge,
the only kind that won't leave a lasting wound in your heart.

＊

When dealing with someone unyielding and difficult,
say to yourself:
"Just like me, he needs to support his family.
Just like me, he's thinking about his future.
Just like me, he must be facing a hardship that
not many people know about."

＊

When someone does something to distress you
for no apparent reason,
or behaves completely unreasonably,
for your own sake, repeat to yourself:
"Big world, some weirdos!"

＊

It's okay for us to disagree.
But if we do, you should say that my opinion
is different from yours, not wrong.
There is a huge difference.
Try putting yourself in my shoes.
How would you feel if you were told
you were wrong just for being different?

＊

It is hard to know things as they really are
because when we hear something,
we rely on past experience to understand it.
Ten people hearing the same story
will each interpret it differently,
since their individual histories lead them to focus on
different aspects.

＊

Each of us has our own unique perspective.
Seen from it, everyone seems to be right.
But if we want to come to an agreement,
rather than asserting our own perspective,
we need to say:
"Your perspective reveals something
that I had been unaware of.
Tell me more, because I want to understand it."
Instead of trying to persuade,
we should first try to understand the other person.

＊

We hurt each other more often through ignorance
than through spite.
If we have hurt each other, say,
"I am very sorry and want to resolve this.
I must have misunderstood you."

*

We often hurt people without knowing it.
Genuine repentance should be directed toward
not only those we have hurt knowingly,
but also the many we have hurt unwittingly.

*

The good driver sees the organic flow
of all the cars on the road
and becomes one with the flow upon joining it.
The bad driver does not see this flow as a whole,
and thinks only of how he himself is driving.

✳

When I feel compelled to interfere
in someone else's business,
I try to ask myself,
"Am I concentrating on the task I have been given?"
When my meditation practice is going well,
I am too busy looking within myself
to bother with other people's affairs.
But when I cannot concentrate on my meditation practice,
my mind starts to wander and notice the faults in others.
And I soon see they are my own faults reflected back at me.
No one has asked me to focus my attention there.
In moments like this,
I recall my original intention of being a monk
and return to my practice.

Chapter Four

RELATIONSHIPS

Since the world is interconnected
and interdependent,
if one of us is in pain, we all feel it.

ON A ZEN RETREAT

Unlike in August, when the autumn meditation retreat began, in September it was quite chilly in the morning and evening at Bongam Zen Monastery. During this retreat period, the monastery housed one hundred monks—slightly more than at normal times—who gathered to meditate for many hours, seated on cushions. At three o'clock every morning, we would get up, wash our faces, and then go to the Buddha hall for the early morning service. While walking to the Buddha hall, I would often be greeted by starlight streaming down from the clear night sky. The refreshing air of Mount Huiyang and the sound of the clear rapid water surrounding the monastery help monks stay alert to the here and now.

During this retreat period, I volunteered for *gansang*, which in Korean means arranging on the table the various dishes made in the kitchen for the formal monastic meal called *baru gongyang*. Since I was the most senior of the seven monks on the *gansang* team, I was asked to be the head. The other monks were sincere and diligent, and when the time came, we were able to carry out our duties well, in a spirit of harmony.

But while we were busy preparing for lunch, I was suddenly called by an older monk, who directed me to leave my team and sweep the outside steps leading down from the kitchen. The moment I heard his instructions, I began to wonder, why did such a task have to fall to our table-setting team? All of us were clearly busy with our own work; it was inconsiderate of the older monk to make us do this extra cleaning, too. And, of course, he would know that people don't like to be told what to do outside their assigned job; if the state of the steps was such a bother to him, why pass the task on to others? He could have cleaned them himself!

After I had finished all the table-setting tasks for lunch, I swept the steps on my own, thinking that someone like this old monk, who dumped whatever tasks he didn't like onto his juniors, should never have become a monk in the first place. But when I finished sweeping the steps, I realized that it had taken me less than five minutes. All that pointless anguish over such a simple task; I could have done it without getting so worked up. All of a sudden I was embarrassed.

WHAT DISTRESSES US IS LESS the circumstances we find ourselves in and more the energy we expend in resisting them. Once we actually do the work, we are often surprised that it was not as hard as we imagined it to be. But when we resist, we become preoccupied by an endless cycle of negative thoughts, and in turn feel harried and stressed.

Of course if someone continuously abuses your goodwill, you should express your feelings. But if you are dealing with a situation that you have no control over, or can't do much to change, then it is better to suspend your internal monologue, which serves only to make you feel irritated and aggrieved. The eminent Zen master Seongcheol (1912–1993) taught us to attain inner peace by not feeding negative thoughts and learning to accept circumstances. We don't need to suffer more by producing unnecessary thoughts.

I HAD ANOTHER SMALL REALIZATION in connection with the monastic meal. Unlike breakfast and lunch, dinner in the monastery is an informal meal, as some monks choose not to eat it, since it can make them drowsy for the evening sitting session. Because it is informal, we sit around simple four-legged tables in order of monastic seniority. This meant that every evening I had to sit opposite the same monk. Unfortunately he was not that friendly, always sitting with an expressionless face. At first I tried to draw him out with a few remarks and questions, hoping to establish a rapport. But he only ever gave the briefest replies to my questions and seemed to be annoyed by my conversation.

As the retreat continued, I would sit in total silence across from the monk, who was more impassive than anyone else at the dinner table. I was uncomfortable the whole time, wondering whether there was something in particular about me that he'd taken a dislike to. But about two weeks later I had a sudden realization—oddly enough, in the library.

The LIBRARY AT BONGAM ZEN Monastery had been built just recently, so only one monk other than myself sought it out in the whole time I was there on retreat. And yet, even while sitting at the same long table, the two of us never so much as exchanged a single glance, much less spoke to each other. When I became aware of this, it struck me that, sitting impassive in the library, I must have looked no different from the monk who sat in silence across from me at every evening meal. And though I might have appeared indifferent or impassive to the monk in the library, this had nothing to do with anything bad I'd heard about him, or any antipathy on my part. I simply had given my full concentration over to the Buddhist texts I was reading; I was thinking absolutely nothing about that other monk, nei-

ther good nor bad. Wasn't it likely, then, that the monk who ate dinner across from me also had no particular regard for me?

Three weeks into the retreat, the opportunity came about, quite by chance, to have tea with the monk who sat opposite me at each evening meal. Seeing him cut a slice of apple and place it in front of me, and address me with a peaceful smile on his face, my realization was confirmed. A person's behavior might not be motivated by any particular thought or feeling, but still we make all kinds of assumptions, deciding, "This person must think x about me." Even though these are just projections of our anxiety onto someone else, we teach ourselves to dislike and even hate them, firmly believing in the truth of our assumptions.

AFTER OUR *GANSANG* TEAM HAD finished cleaning up and putting bowls away after lunch, we took a leisurely stroll across a field of beautiful pine trees against the backdrop of scenic mountains. All of a sudden, a feeling of gratitude and peace came over me: I was free of thoughts and simply appreciated everything around me in that moment. Unlike the chilly September mornings, the daytime still held the warmth of late summer.

＊

Living with family, friends, or roommates
can be as difficult as doing spiritual practice,
requiring you to act in consideration of others
by either renouncing or moderating your desires.
Not criticizing those who live a different way than you do
and making an effort to understand and accept them,
that, too, is an important part of spiritual practice.

＊

There are times when you assume the worst
about someone and break off your relationship for good.
At such times, stop for a moment.
Fight the impulse to have the last word
and to make an irrevocable break,
lest you regret your decision, thinking,
"I should have kept my mouth shut."

＊

We all wish to belong.
It is through those who care deeply about us
that we find love and purpose in our lives.
After all, we are all imperfect beings who need one another.

*

If you're really drawn to someone,
do not try to control them.
Just try to enjoy spending time together.
Only then will you be able to meet again.
When you do not try to possess someone
and just enjoy their company,
the connection endures.

*

It's best for two people
to be equally drawn to each other.
If one person likes the other too intensely, too soon,
it can be scary, burdensome, or annoying.

*

Two people can have a great first impression of each other,
only for the relationship to quickly go bad.
Rather than having seen each other
for who they are,
they only saw a fantasy
that they projected onto each other.

＊

If you have a friend whom you have
suddenly grown very close to, be careful!
If you make a mistake, such a friend
can easily turn into an enemy.
When you are so close
that you feel there is nothing you cannot say,
you can easily hurt each other.

＊

If you suddenly become close to someone
and start spending a lot of time together,
you can come to dislike each other just as suddenly.
You may start to feel that
the other person is imprisoning you
or that they take you for granted.
It takes time to develop trust and affection.
Wait until you actually miss each other
before meeting up again.

*

People who do not make an effort
to form or maintain a relationship,
thinking that it will happen if it's meant to,
often remain single.
The person you are "destined" for
will not suddenly appear one day,
knocking on your door,
like in the French film *Amélie.*
One cannot become president
without campaigning,
even someone with a great chance of winning.
A good relationship will never come about
without work.

*

You like someone,
but he doesn't like you back;
he likes you, but you think he is just so-so;
you like each other, but those around you get in the way.
Having a relationship with someone is not easy.
But if you do not give up, and keep working at it,
at just the right season, the relationship will happen.

*

"Sunim, I finally figured it out.
The success rate for meeting the right person
is one in ten.
Only after you have met nine other people
does one appear who you like
and who also likes you back."

*

Perhaps there is no such thing as a "soul mate."
When you work hard to make your relationship work
and stay together for a long time,
then you each become the person
you were meant to be with.

*

If there is someone you genuinely love,
whisper this to them this evening.
I love you more than myself.
I love you more than yesterday.
You are where my heart starts from each morning.

*

If you finally manage to meet up with someone
after trying for a week or a month,
the meeting will feel meaningful
in proportion to the time you had to wait.
In this fast-paced world, where so much gets done
immediately,
when you have to wait long enough for anticipation to build,
the moment with that person will be very special.

*

If you really like someone,
you do not offer the excuse that you are busy.
No matter how busy you are,
you still make time.
If he constantly makes excuses,
let him go.
You deserve better than him.

*

After every date, do you feel a little hurt?
Why do you think that is?
Maybe because you like him more than he likes you?
If that is the case, then distance yourself from him
and turn your attention to your own work.
If it is a true relationship, he will come back to you.

*

There is nothing more foolish
than obsessing over someone who doesn't like you
and believing you can change that person's mind.
Please, let the person go.
If you do,
someone else will come into your life.

*

It was very painful to break up with him, right?
But, looking back at it with a clear head,
you knew from the start
that he was not a good match.

*

The more expectations you have for a relationship,
the more likely it is to go awry.
When a relationship feels difficult, examine it closely.
Might it be that one of you is expecting too much?

*

If you are going to think,
"Why don't they do for me
as much as I have done for them?"
then do not do it in the first place.
Or give only so much that you won't expect
something in return.
If you feel the need to have a gesture reciprocated,
the relationship will start to feel uncomfortable.

*

We can get hurt by our family and friends
because we rely on them excessively,
or are overly involved in their lives.
Demanding too much, or having too much
demanded of you, is not healthy.
A relationship has to be tended to like a fire:
If someone comes too close, tell her to take a step back.

✳

Obsession feels a lot like love.
But of course it is not love.
With obsession, unlike with love,
you feel the subtle selfish desire
to manipulate the other person
according to your wishes.
While love lets the other person be,
obsession wants control.

✳

When a problem comes up in a relationship,
don't just grit your teeth and bear it.
Acknowledge that the other person
can be different from you,
and allow them to be.
Even siblings who have grown up in the same house
have different viewpoints and habits.
Do not just tell them to adjust to you;
make room for difference.

✳

At first you found him interesting
and even exciting because he is different from you.
Now that difference is precisely
what makes your relationship hard, isn't it?

*

You have come to hate
the one you used to love so much.
At such a moment, recognize
how fleeting love is,
how slippery are the whims of our heart,
how conditional love can be.

*

Remember this:
What heart-throbbing love brings with it—
hatred and jealousy, longing and sadness,
even loathing and regret—
are all just passengers on the same ship.

*

How someone speaks
about the other relationships they've had
before meeting you
tells you how they will speak
about you to other people
whenever your relationship hits
even a small bump in the road.

Do not think of yourself as a crescent moon,
waiting for someone else to fill in the missing part of you.
When you stand alone like a full moon, already
complete in yourself,
you will meet another person who is whole and
complete just like you,
and between you two, a healthy relationship can grow.
Do not try to fit yourselves to each other
to make one whole moon.
Instead, be more like two full moons.
You'll respect each other's individuality and interests
while creating a relationship in which each of you
shines brightly on the other.

DEALING WITH DISAPPOINTMENT

MANY PEOPLE ANSWER THE QUESTION "What is the most difficult thing in life?" with "Relationships." Since it takes two people to make a relationship work, and a relationship can easily be disrupted by third parties, relationships are tricky things to nurture. In my own experience, even relationships that were strong for a long time seemed to suffer when, unbeknownst to myself, I started to feel disappointed in the other person. Whenever I feel disappointed, if I don't address the feeling, it always comes back to harm the relationship. In other words, a feeling of disappointment is like a warning light, telling me that if I don't do something about it, the relationship could fail.

But unlike other emotions, disappointment is very tricky to express: It comes out as petty and small-minded, whereas if I keep it bottled up, it only gets worse. All of which makes it difficult to act either way. If we are depressed, we can at least say so and ask for help. Similarly, if we feel sad, we can cry. But if we are disappointed, the feeling is harder to express because we have to explain it to the person who has disappointed us.

People who come to me for advice on this describe their experience of disappointment in various ways. When parents fail to keep a promise, their children feel disappointed—say, if their father was supposed to take them out to play or come to a school performance, but he forgot. Many fathers I've spoken with have shared their feelings of disappointment upon being treated like they are invisible by their wives and children. The same feelings arise in a wife when her husband does not take her side in a disagreement with her in-laws or friends. A young man or woman in a relationship can feel disappointed when the partner who has been so attentive gradually becomes halfhearted, not even responding when spoken to. Office workers can feel disappointment, too, when colleagues or subordinates do not respect their ideas, or when a boss does not say anything about a project they've worked overtime on.

Our feelings of disappointment stem from having expectations of another person that go unfulfilled. Such expectations are often unspoken, and yet we wish that people would somehow figure them out based on nonverbal clues and fulfill them for us. When they're not met, we become frustrated and want to shout, "Do I have to spell it out every time? Why can't you figure out what I want by looking at me and my circumstances?" But of course it is difficult to know exactly what someone else expects if they haven't told us. Without the power of telepathy, how can we know what someone else is expecting?

If we do not express our feelings of disappointment, they will start to build up and transform into more difficult emotions, such as anger, hurt, or even betrayal, and we may come to hold a grudge. So it is best to share your disappointment, rather than leaving it to build up inside you. And when you express it, you should be careful not to do so in a way that is aggressive or critical of the other person, or when the other person is angry. Instead, wait until both of you are calm and composed, and talk about only how you feel right then, not what was done or said many years ago. It can feel awkward at first, but after a bit of practice you will be able to stop repressing these feelings, and speak calmly without damaging your relationship.

FINALLY, if you seem to have feelings of disappointment more often than others, it is time to look more closely at yourself. When you feel disappointed, and you see it's because you expected something from someone else, consider why it is that you often rely on others to make you happy. Why is your self-reliance so low? Does it maybe relate to how you were brought up, or to a past trauma? Do you have a strong need for approval or attention from others? If you often feel disappointed in yourself, ask why you hold yourself to such a high standard. Are your expectations reasonable? When you understand yourself better, you might find it easier to deal with disappointment, and to accept and love yourself.

＊

Try to share your true feelings.
Even if the other person is hurt at first,
eventually she will be grateful to know the truth.
The truth is freeing
to both the one who expresses it
and the one who hears it.

＊

True friends and good colleagues
are not those who say only pleasant things to you.
When it's clear you have made a mistake,
they will tell you that you are at fault.

＊

Do not complain that someone has not
accommodated your every desire.
The real problem may be your expectation
that others must adapt to you.
The person who always adapts to you?
There is no such saint in the world.

*

Much of the stress in relationships
comes from the lack of communication.
If you stop talking to each other,
your hearts will grow distant,
and you will misunderstand each other.
In your relationships with family, partners, and friends,
however angry you may be,
do not let the rope of conversation
go slack for very long.

*

There are times when someone wants to talk
and you give them the cold shoulder.
But the longer this goes on,
the more it exacerbates the problem.
And there are times when you deliberately
avoid talking to someone,
but they don't even notice.
Ultimately you are the only one who suffers.
For your own sake, start talking.
The silent treatment rarely works.

*

A good job and money are important to our well-being.
But when our relationships are harmonious,
and we feel appreciated and accepted,
that is when we feel most peaceful and content.

*

We often feel happiest when we forget ourselves.
When we feel grateful for someone,
we think about that person, not so much about ourselves.
When we most enjoy dancing, we lose ourselves in it.
But when we are constantly thinking about ourselves,
we become overly self-conscious and even egotistical.

*

Recall one person whom you were grateful to recently.
Send her a thank-you email or text message right now.
While you write it,
you will notice your heart feels warm and happy.
And if you wait a little,
you will soon receive a reply
that will be sure to make you smile.

＊

If you buy a new year's calendar or diary,
write the name of each person
you are close to next to their birthday.
And when their birthday comes,
contact them to wish them well.
The root of happiness
lies in deep and lasting relationships.

＊

I don't think life has something grand in store for me.
Everyday interactions with people
are the very stuff of my life.
And so I have to treat those around me as precious,
because other than myself,
they are the main characters in my life story.

＊

Ultimately we desire to go beyond our ego,
and to feel at one with the universe.
That's why sharing makes us happy—
it increases our feeling of connection.
So if you want to be happier and more connected,
instead of accumulating things, let them circulate back
into the universe and see what happens.
Something new and good will flow back to you.

＊

If you want to excel in a relationship,
the way to do so is very simple:
Give more than you receive.
The more we receive, we can't help but
feel grateful and like the person.

＊

If you want a more harmonious relationship,
stop monitoring who owes what.
If you constantly think,
"Why did they not give me as much as I gave them?"
you are constantly impeding
the natural flow of your relationship.

＊

Before asking someone for a favor,
a wise person thinks about
how to help that person first.
A foolish person asks a favor thoughtlessly.
He talks about powerful people he knows,
or tries to make you feel a sense of obligation,
or else he simply begs again and again.

＊

If someone did not ask for your help,
do not try to solve her problem for her.
Though your intention may be good,
you risk taking control away from her
and injuring her self-esteem.

＊

When a family conflict comes up,
don't take sides;
just listen to what both sides have to say.
Otherwise you will only make the problem worse
and risk hurting a family member without meaning to.

If your current circumstances
     are stressful,
try visualizing this:
Your circumstances are a
     hurricane,
and you are the eye of the
     storm.
Do not get swept away by the
     storm.
Follow the wisdom
emanating from the storm's
     peaceful eye.

*

The reason we think we are better than others
is that inferiority still lurks within us.
A sense of superiority exists
because of a sense of inferiority.

*

In the course of our lives, we meet people
who aggravate our sense of inferiority:
the friend with a more successful career,
the colleague with a better education and looks,
the in-laws with a lot more money.
But look beyond these externals.
People who seem better off
have other difficulties,
brought on by the very things
you envy them for.

*

Someone's true self cannot be known
by the things that are easy to judge,
like physical appearance, academic degree, job title, etc.
Those things don't tell us whether someone is
humorous, kind, considerate, good at keeping promises,
generous toward subordinates or those less fortunate.
Only when we know these kinds of things
can we come to understand who they really are.

*

You can impress someone with words at first,
but without actions to back them up,
the good feeling cannot last.

*

Who is an unfortunate person?
One who looks at other people and sees only their flaws.

*

If you listen to someone tell a story about someone else,
in many cases more is revealed about the speaker than
the one they are speaking about.
Of all the attributes that make up a person,
they are speaking of the one that captured their attention.

*

If someone who has never met you
says this and that about you,
tossing off observations quite easily,
then it's clear what is really happening:
They are just projecting.

When we tried to talk critically
about someone whom everyone at the meeting knew,
an elder monk stood up and said:
"What is the point of talking about someone
who is not here?"

*

There are times when a story
that begins, "This is a secret . . ."
is not really a secret, or not your secret to tell.
If it's the former, then you are hoping to win
the confidence of your listener.
If the latter, then you must want to feel
the pleasure of disclosure.

*

When you are with one friend,
you end up gossiping about celebrities;
with another, you speak about money;
with another, politics;
and with yet another, spirituality.
This is because, rather than
"you" being something fixed,
you change moment to moment,
depending on whom you are with.
In light of this,
cultivate a deeper connection with those people
in whose company you like yourself best.

*

Sushi tastes better with a cup of green tea.
But if you eat it with Coca-Cola,
it doesn't taste as good.
The right combination is a key to success.

When you have experienced something deeply unfair,
make a formal complaint at least once, if not twice,
so that it won't happen to other people.
And then let the whole thing go, as quickly as possible.
But if you hold on to the memory of it,
you may let new opportunities and experiences pass you by.
With a new heart, focus on the present, not the past.

*

Relationship problems are difficult to resolve.
He is unlikely to change to suit you;
she won't be quick to forgive
all the accumulated hurt.
It seems all we can do
is try to understand the other person—
the circumstances we weren't aware of
that make them act the way they do.
The problem doesn't go away
as soon as you figure things out,
but as you come to some degree of understanding,
you discover your own heart,
softer and more open than before.

Chapter Five

COURAGE

When the waves of an ordeal roll in,
do not act out of desperation.
Instead, go to a peaceful place
and dwell on the silence within yourself.
When your mind touches its deep silence,
you realize that you have enough
inner strength and wisdom
to go through with this.

TO MY BELOVED
YOUNG FRIENDS

MY DEAR BELOVED YOUNG FRIENDS: Each time I see your slumped shoulders, each time I hear your listless voices, my heart aches. How are you these days? Did you have another long day at school or work? It seems no one has told you that if you're courageous, you can create your own destiny; it is entirely up to you to decide what kind of life you would like to have. Instead, you have been told by your parents and teachers that you should just follow the norm and do what the world expects of you. If you say that you want to become a musician or an artist, if you want to travel the world, if you want to have a serious relationship, you might be told: "Now is not the right time. You should concentrate on your studies." When you started college, you thought you could finally have the life you wanted. But then what happened? You were told to prepare for your career. You had to apply for summer internships and study for qualifying exams. Again you were bombarded with reasons to delay your own life.

WE HAVE BECOME ACCUSTOMED TO sacrificing the present for the sake of the future. We consider it a matter of course that the present just has to be put up with until one day that bright future arrives. We have overlooked the importance of enjoying the journey while prizing only the destination. But in the course of our lives, there comes a time when we begin to doubt whether this present that we are enduring will ever lead to the future of our dreams. Even if the dream comes true, will it be worth the sacrifice we made to our relationships and health and happiness in order to achieve it? And what if the dream we achieved was never ours but that of our parents or teachers? What if we were just measuring ourselves against society's yardstick of success?

Even if we are lucky enough to get a job at our dream company, we will be starting out in an entry-level position, and it might be hard to find senior colleagues who value our perspective. It's only natural that we won't get everything right at first, as we are still learning. And when we don't know how to do something, we will want our colleagues to teach us, patiently—but they only look irritated and reproach us for being incompetent. Soon we will start doubting whether we are right for the job, whether we ought to dedicate our life to this place just to make our parents proud.

I was not very different from you. In fact, when I was in high school I was depressed and unhappy. I was told that if I got accepted to a good college, I would be seen as a success by my family and friends. I would be respected by society, and a nice job would be waiting for me. I craved that acknowledgment and respect. My family had always been poor, and I thought I could change that if only I studied hard enough and threw myself into my schoolwork more intensely than those around me. And although that wasn't such a terrible life, if I look back and ask myself what exactly I gained from studying for so many years for my Ph.D., the honest answer is nothing more than the somewhat deflating realization of what it's like to be an academic—and that the answers to my questions about the mysteries of life are not to be found in academia. In that sense, you could say that my greatest gain was the knowledge that I was not living the life that I hoped for.

Many people have asked me, "How did you find the courage to become a monk?" Well, I didn't want to waste my life anymore wondering whether it tallied with some socially determined criteria for success. I got tired of trying to satisfy other people's expectations. Instead, I wanted to discover for myself the answers to questions like "Why was I born?" and "What happens when I die?" I longed to experience enlightenment according to what the Buddha taught. I wanted to meditate more and live simply with like-minded folks. Looked at one way, my decision might seem self-centered, and in another way, like a brave choice. But just once, for just one moment in my life, I had to try to live a life without regret. Even if others scorn me and mock my decision, only having done it can I look at myself and say with confidence that I have loved my life.

My beloved young friends: It's okay to live the life that you wish for. You are allowed to create your own destiny, free from the expectations of your parents and society. You can live the life you yourself think has meaning. Even if those around you try to dissuade you, saying you can't, you mustn't, it won't work, they are not living your life for you, are they?

Many people who try to forge their own path or strike out for uncharted territory come up against strong opposition. If your timid heart wonders, "Is this really okay?" have the courage to smile back at your heart and say firmly, "Yes, it is!" Even if you fail, you will learn from your mistakes and try it differently next time. Besides, it is better to experience failure while you are still young. As long as you are prepared to take responsibility for the consequences of your choices, you can follow your heart. Wouldn't you want to grasp the wheel of your life and live as the master of your destiny? I hope that you can break free from self-imposed limits and discover the courage to finally change your life.

*

There are times when things are going well for you,
and people offer you unsolicited advice in the name of love.
They tell you to think about financial security, marriage,
your future.
At such times, do not be shaken. Just keep walking the path
you have chosen, like the steadfast march of elephants.

*

Don't assume another bus will be coming.
Sometimes the route will have changed,
and you will never get another chance
to catch the bus you missed.
If an opportunity is presented to you,
don't give in to your fear.
Muster your courage and get on that bus.

*

If you've waited for someone to show up
and change your life,
and they still haven't appeared, don't wait any longer.
It probably means you need
to become that person for yourself.
When you feel like relying on someone else, remember:
There lives a far stronger and wiser being inside you than
you imagine.

＊

Ask yourself:
What are the values that guide my life?
What do I want to achieve in my life?
If the answer is clear, you can live more confidently,
knowing your life's direction
and that you are not mindlessly following the herd.

＊

If you just go along with the crowd
without trying to figure out
what you really want to do,
you'll likely wind up striving to succeed
in a highly competitive profession.
Then, after several years of stress and struggle,
you might become depressed from continuing to fall short
in auditions, job interviews, or qualification tests.
There are more than thirty thousand kinds
of jobs in the world.
If you want to succeed, be more self-aware
about your values, interests, strengths, and limitations,
and explore professions beyond those you are familiar with.
You won't regret taking the time to do this.

*

When you try to learn something new,
you will inevitably feel embarrassed in the process.
No matter how respected you are in your own field,
you will be treated like a kid
and corrected every time you do it wrong.
If you cannot stand to make mistakes,
you will never be able to learn a foreign language, a sport,
a musical instrument, or how to drive or cook.

*

If you don't feel like studying,
start with the subject you like best.
If a meal looks unappealing,
start with what looks tastiest.
It's all right to start reading a book
from the section you most want to read.
Starting is often the most difficult part.
Once you have started,
it's much easier to continue.

＊

New ideas often come from the margins,
where people question and challenge the norms
set by the mainstream.
Rather than lamenting that you're an outsider,
use your unique position to your advantage
and create something original and interesting.

＊

Michel Foucault, Jacques Derrida, Edward Said—
celebrated twentieth-century thinkers—
all started out discriminated against.
Michel Foucault was gay.
Jacques Derrida was from Algeria.
Edward Said was a Palestinian in Egypt
with an American passport.
Instead of seeing their outsider status as a disadvantage,
they used their unique perspectives
to revolutionize Western philosophy.

＊

Excessive thought won't solve a problem.
Rather than trying to fix it by thinking,
set your mind at ease.
A solution will rise to the surface.
Remember that wisdom comes from stillness.

*

When you have too much to worry about,
ask yourself: "Am I solving anything by worrying?"
Because of your worries, are you missing out on the present?
If worrying is not doing any good, say to your anxious mind,
"If what I'm worried about actually happens,
that's when I will worry!"

*

Are you suffering from anxiety?
Try prioritizing your worries by writing them down.
If something you're worried about hasn't happened yet,
put it at the end of the list.
Worry only about the problems facing you right now;
for the rest, you can cross that bridge when you come to it.

*

Thinking too much can make it difficult to act.
If you just do it, then it is done.
But if you give in to your thinking,
your mind will get in the way,
telling you "you can't," "you shouldn't," "you don't want to."
In that case, get up early the next morning
and just do the thing you've been putting off.
If you give yourself time to start thinking about it,
inaction will take hold again.

*

Even if it's not perfect,
set it aside and move on to the next thing.
The idea of "perfection" exists only in your mind,
and may not be the same for everyone.

*

Before an exam or interview, always remember:
You know so much more than you think you do.
Our unconscious contains an ocean of wisdom.
Have confidence in yourself.

*

Distinguish between the things you can control
and those you can't.
For instance, the past cannot be undone.
You cannot control what other people think of you.
But you can control what you are doing right now.
The way to be free of worry and anxiety
is to focus your attention on the present moment.

*

Do not be afraid of making mistakes.
Be afraid only of not learning from your mistakes.
An expert is someone who has acquired skills and knowledge
by making a lot of mistakes.

My youth was the most
difficult
time for me.
I constantly had to
prove myself
because the older
generation saw me

only as young and
inexperienced.
But there is a light at the end
of the tunnel.
It will reveal itself not
suddenly but gradually.
Don't be discouraged. Things
will get better for sure.

THE FIRST FAILURE

"Haemin Sunim, I didn't get into a good college. I'm so embarrassed by what a failure I am. I don't know what to do."

"I spent a whole year preparing for the bar exam but didn't pass, while many of my friends did. I should probably take it again, but I feel like just giving up."

"I quit my job and opened a shop, but things didn't turn out as I expected. There were barely any customers, so I had to close up after six months. I've lost face in front of my family, and hit rock bottom financially. It's making me depressed and scared."

The first failure is always incredibly painful. And most of us are rarely prepared for it. The exam is very difficult, but somehow we think we will pass. Or, although the economy is not so good these days, we think that as long as we work hard, the shop will somehow be a success. But only when we fail do we realize we did not have a backup plan. Especially for those who put all their effort into achieving a certain goal only to come up short, the future can seem very bleak. If their life's journey has been fairly smooth up to that point, their failure will feel like a wake-up call to a harsh reality.

But failure is bound to happen again and again throughout our lives. And there will be countless plans that won't turn out as we had hoped. In other words, the failure is a very common experience, even though it may not feel that way. It is important not to beat ourselves up or consider our lives a big failure. Instead, we should accept the fact that things didn't work out this time, and look carefully at where we went wrong. Once we have a clear understanding of what happened, we can resolve to avoid making the same mistakes and to move forward with our lives. Otherwise, there is a good chance we will fail again in exactly the same way.

IT MAY SOUND SILLY FOR A MONK to have trouble finding a job, but I experienced my first major failure in the process of becoming a professor in the United States. After finishing my Ph.D., I applied to teach at various colleges and universities; luckily, there were six schools where I passed both the first round, document screening, and the second round, a conference interview. For the final round, I was invited to campus for two days for more interviews and to present in front of students and faculty. Unfortunately, among the six, the one college that I had my heart set on was the quickest to reject me after the campus interview. I'd never experienced failure like that before, and it hurt and frustrated me deeply. Even though I had three other campus interviews remaining, the knowledge that I had failed to get this job made me start to doubt my abilities and to think about giving up the whole thing. I was getting depressed, and all I wanted to do was sleep.

But after a few days of sleeping, something within me woke me up early in the morning and made me examine why I had failed to land that job. Initially, before going to the campus interviews, I believed that if I were to put in an honest effort and show my sincerity and preparedness, I would probably be hired. But on that early morning, it dawned on me that this approach was simply wrong. What the college had wanted was not the most sincere candidate doing his best, but the one who already possessed the abilities to meet the position's particular needs. In other words, I had been naïve and complacent in anticipating just what it was that the college wanted from its new faculty. The starting point should have never been myself but the needs of the college. From then on, I prepared for the remaining interviews by thoroughly researching what each college was looking for. This soon paid off with an offer of employment from one of them.

DID YOU FAIL AT A JOB INTERVIEW? Instead of settling for the vague hope that things will be okay if you just try harder next time, figure out exactly where you went wrong, and don't repeat the same mistake again. Are you at a loss because you did not score high enough on a standardized test such as the SAT, bar exam, or CPA exam? Then take a close look at your study habits. Did you study in a distracting place? Did you make a study schedule and stick to it? Did you ever ask for advice from people who scored high on the test? If you're frustrated because your business went under, don't waste time assigning blame; take responsibility and calmly ask why you failed. Did you choose the wrong location for the shop? Were your products not sufficiently unique or of high enough quality? Did you go wrong in your relationships with customers, staff, or business partners? If you decide to start another business, spend double, even triple the amount of time you did before on research and building a business plan.

Failure is something we all experience. Each time we fail, we can learn from our mistakes and become a little bit wiser and more prudent. Failure can also be an opportunity to rethink our lives and grow mentally and spiritually. I wish you the best of luck in your next endeavor.

Frustration and failure are a part of life.
If we do not flee from them but accept them calmly,
we come to know what we need to do next.

✳

Just because you have failed to achieve your goal,
it does not mean all your efforts were in vain.
Failure is meaningful in itself,
teaching you many new things.
No one can tell the sum of a life until it has come to its end.

✳

You have not screwed up your life
just because you screwed up an exam.
Nor is your life a failure
just because your business failed.
When you have had a negative experience,
be wary of thoughts that
make it seem worse than it is.

✳

The first step to overcoming failure
is to fully admit you have failed.
Admitting it will put your mind at ease
and help you to see what you ought to do next.

✳

Having too much success too young
is one of life's greatest perils.
Don't try to climb higher than you can go before you're ready.
You will get there step-by-step.

＊

When something hasn't turned out well,
don't give up; keep going,
and try different ways of making it work.
There is no fixed answer, no single solution.
We find the best approach through trial and error.

＊

After rolling thunder and a torrential downpour,
we can see the blue sky and green mountains
so much clearer and brighter than before.
And after experiencing a great trial,
we come to see clearly what is truly important in our lives.

＊

"Life isn't about waiting for the storm to pass.
It's about learning to dance in the rain."
—Vivian Greene

＊

Don't be disheartened, my friend.
When we look at our lives as a whole,
our current difficulty is like a cloud.
Although large, it will soon pass.

*

When you hope for someone to appear
to solve your problem,
remember that nothing in this world is free.
After solving your problem,
that person often becomes your new problem.

*

Do not beg for people's attention.
As you discover and develop your unique strengths,
they will pay attention to you automatically.
If you catch yourself desiring people's attention,
tell yourself, "I just have to get better at what I do."
You are noble; don't act like a beggar.

*

If you allow yourself to be shaken,
the world will shake you all the harder.
Be like the rock, which is not easily moved
by other people's praise or criticism.

✳

Even when you have tried your absolute best,
someone might still be critical or snide.
There are all kinds of people in this world,
even those who think
the food of a three-Michelin-star chef is just so-so.
No matter who you are, it is impossible for you to please
everyone.

✳

We are far more affected by one word of criticism
than by ten words of praise.
Whenever you are hurt by someone's criticism,
remember that behind that one word of criticism,
there are ten words of praise—
from those who like you and cheer you on.

✳

If we see someone passionate about his work,
we naturally feel drawn to him.
As he is completely absorbed in his work,
we can't take our eyes off of him.
Passion is contagious.

*

If someone is promoting a product
but doesn't fully believe in it, it will not sell.
It is not the product that sells but the seller's passion.

*

Have you ever tried your best to the point of tears?
No one else may know, but you know that you really did
your best.
Even if you fail, you will have nothing to regret.

*

If heaven wants you to grow,
it sends one rival who is more capable than you
and has a better background and a nicer personality.
As you compete with your rival,
you discover different abilities lying dormant inside you.
Although you might have hated your rival,
when you look back and see
how much you grew during that time,
you will probably feel grateful to him.

*

Try solving this riddle:
"Do you know which role
is the most difficult one in your company?"
Answer: "The role I am assigned to."

＊

Do not try to demonstrate how smart you are
by nitpicking people's faults
that are too minor even to mention.
It will be obvious what you are doing.

＊

Do not try to promote yourself
by criticizing people ahead of you.
If you do, you, too, will be criticized
by those behind you.
Instead, try to win recognition
through your own hard work and talent.
The moment you attack someone,
your true worth is revealed.

＊

It's a mistake to assume
that everything about your dream job
will be fun and interesting.
All jobs have their tedious aspects.
Know that there are always trials to get through
before something bears fruit.

＊

I thought that professors just taught and did research.
But after becoming a professor,
I realized that the work involves
all sorts of things I didn't care for,
like collecting receipts,
writing recommendation letters,
filling out applications and reports for research grants,
giving lectures to prospective students and their parents, etc.
This seems to be the case with every kind of work.
You get to do what you like
if you also do what you don't like.

＊

When the time comes to do a task
you have anticipated doing for a long time,
you assume you will be quite nervous.
But if you've prepared to the best of your ability,
you become unexpectedly calm, not too nervous.
Knowing that you can now show
how hard you have been working,
you even become somewhat excited.
If you've prepared thoroughly,
there's nothing to be nervous about.

＊

"Put your heart, mind, and soul
into even your smallest acts.
This is the secret of success."
—SWAMI SIVANANDA

＊

It seems we acquire the most strength and wisdom
at those points in our lives that are the most difficult.
Later on, we think back on those difficult times,
on what we learned from them
and how we came through them.
Then we realize that they have been
a priceless experience for us.

Say "So what?" to the part of yourself
that feels nervous and inferior.
"I'm a bit nervous about the exam. So what?"
"I'm shorter and heavier than the others. So what?"
"I don't have much money in the bank. So what?"
Once you have acknowledged your insecurities like this,
you will find the courage within to overcome them.
If you try to conceal the inferior part of yourself
while feeling ashamed of it, it will continue to be a problem.
No one really cares about it if you are comfortable with it.

Chapter Six

HEALING

May my own pain open my heart
wide enough to embrace others in pain.
May my suffering become
an opportunity to connect with others who are suffering.
Just as I wish for
a swift end to my suffering,
I also pray for others
to recover quickly from their pain.

WHEN FORGIVENESS IS HARD

IN EACH OF OUR LIVES, there will be someone who does something absolutely unforgivable. We know we ought to forgive them for our own sake, rather than remain filled with hatred and rage, but that's easier said than done. How can we so easily forgive someone who has told such awful lies about us, leaving us feeling hurt and insulted? They have stepped over us on their way to the top and stabbed us in the back. Each time we see them, they act as though they have done nothing of the sort. The wound is so deep that we are not sure whether we will ever be able to heal.

At times like these, we should try not to forgive the person too quickly. The first step to healing a deep emotional wound is to recognize and accept our feelings for what they are: burning rage and intense hatred. These are the mind's natural attempt to draw a clear boundary between the person and ourselves. They function as a protective wall, allowing our vulnerable selves to heal. If someone encourages us to set aside that rage before we are ready, we run the risk of deepening the wound by breaking the protective wall too soon.

But it can be a problem if the memory keeps rising up even after many years have passed, leaving us trapped like a hamster on a wheel, unable to move on from the pain. The more we remember how the pain came about, the more we come to despise ourselves for not having stood up for ourselves. As our mind dwells on the past, we also fail to notice what the present moment is offering us and cannot fully enjoy our lives. Even though our mind resolves to forgive, our heart stays stubbornly closed. Worse, because no one ever taught us the practical steps to take to be able to forgive someone, there is an unbridgeable gulf between head and heart, and this becomes yet another source of distress.

One Sunday evening, I had dinner with an old high school friend whom I had been very close to. We hadn't been in touch since our high school graduation, but he'd reached out after discovering that I had become a monk. Although it was a little awkward at first, as we had spent many years leading different lives, it didn't take long to feel comfortable again. He was from a poor family just like I was, but worked harder than anyone I knew. He did his best not only in his classes, but also with extracurricular activities like sports and music. He had gone to a top university, then landed a job at one of the best companies in Korea. After working at that company for about ten years, he started his own firm. Everyone regarded him as a success.

After we had finished eating, my friend, as though he had been biding his time throughout the meal, suddenly blurted out: "Please help me, Haemin Sunim. Lately I've been a bit depressed, and don't feel like doing anything. It's all become too much." My successful, hardworking friend sat there with his shoulders slumped and his face looking like that of a young boy. Having intuited what things had been like for him at home, I spoke carefully. "You've always worked so hard, ever since you were a child; why do you think that is?" At first he spoke of the obligations of being the breadwinner, and then, as I continued to gently press the question, he returned to the subject of his childhood.

"Things at home were pretty tough. If I didn't work hard, it seemed my mother would always have a hard life, so I guess that's why I did it." I continued to draw him out. "Is that it? You just wanted to make things easier for your mother?" At that, his face darkened. He was clearly embarrassed. "Actually, it was my aunt, the wife of my dead father's older brother; I hated how she always looked down on my mother, saying that someone so poor and uneducated would never make a better life for herself and her children. And so to prove her wrong, I was determined to work harder and become more successful than any of my cousins."

"So, each time you saw your mother being slighted by your aunt, you must have felt angry and humiliated. If I'd had an aunt like that, I would have hated her, too. If you really want my help, please try this. First imagine now that this aunt, who hurt you and your mother, is in front of you. Go back to being the child who was wounded, and speak your mind to your aunt. But instead of using the language of an adult, talk as a ten-year-old would. We are returning to the time of your youth. Set aside the importance of respecting your elders, and of not using bad language, and just speak whatever words happen to rise up inside you. Just as they are."

ONE OF THE REASONS why forgiveness is so hard is that our heart does not listen to our mind. We don't know how to connect the two. Sometimes we try to deny or suppress the rage and hatred, hoping they'll go away, but they always come back. Interestingly, however, it is those emotions of rage and hatred that function as the vital conduit through which the mind's decision to forgive reaches the heart. Rather than fight our feelings, we should honor them by allowing them to be there and witnessing how their energy moves inside us. Does it manifest as a flushed face, muscle tension, or elevated heartbeat? Without identifying with the emotions, observe them in a detached yet caring way. Like a mother looking at her child, we can observe our emotions attentively and compassionately.

If we continue to do this, something unexpected happens. Like a layer of an onion skin peeling off, the inner landscape of our emotions begins to reveal itself. In my case, I was able to detect deep sadness beneath the rage, and then, looking even more deeply and compassionately, I discovered the fear of loneliness and death right underneath the sadness. If we can teach ourselves to look at our emotional wounds with curiosity and compassion, our hardened heart will, mysteriously enough, begin to melt.

Once we feel our heart starting to open, we can try directing our compassionate gaze toward the one who wounded us. Try to look deeply and understand their pain and suffering. If they were happy, it's highly unlikely they would have done such a thing to us. See what lies beneath their unhappiness. The aim of this practice is not to excuse the wrongs that were done to us but to untie the knot of our own emotions, which are holding us back and preventing us from living a full life.

In other words, we try to forgive not for the sake of the aggressor but to free ourselves from the past. In order to achieve this, it is important that we try to understand that person.

If we can set aside our judgment and look at the person in the spirit of understanding, we start to see things that hadn't been visible before. For example, inside the boastful figure who looked down on us is a soul that had itself been looked down on. The person may have been ridiculed by their parents, siblings, or friends. The one who hurt me may have behaved the way they did because their life was every bit as lonely and insecure as mine. Facing such a deep truth, our hearts soften unwittingly. If we continue to open our heart to all the other people who are lonely and insecure, and feel how their suffering is just the same as our own, the sorrow inside us transforms into compassion for everyone in the world, including ourselves.

My friend had been silent for a while. As I encouraged him to give voice to what was inside him, he began to wail, venting his long-suppressed rage. "Damn you, damn you!" Like a child, he buried his face in my shoulder and sobbed. "I was so sad for my mom and so angry at my aunt. It was too hard." I shed tears with him. After crying for a while, he seemed to calm down a little and said to me: "That's it, the reason my life has been such a struggle—it's all because I wanted revenge on my aunt, and at the same time to win her recognition. But after she passed away last year, that possibility disappeared, and that's when everything started to feel so empty."

A few days after our dinner, my friend sent me an email, thanking me and telling me that he now felt much more at ease. "It seems I can finally forgive my aunt," he wrote. "I went home and, just as you advised, thought about what kind of suffering my aunt might have endured. It struck me that she had had an unhappy life herself. Her husband was successful, but he constantly cheated on her. Feelings of betrayal and loneliness dominated her married life. If she had been happy, she probably never would have behaved like that to my mother. It feels like I might be able to forgive my aunt and let go of my past."

THERE IS NOT ONLY RAGE and hatred inside us, but also sadness and grief, loneliness and terror. But that is not all. There is also the compassionate inner eye looking at such emotions with equanimity. When you are suffering because someone is hard to forgive, I pray that you find the compassionate gaze inside you.

May you find the eye of
compassion within you!

✳

Underneath someone's violent nature,
there is always fear, rooted in
either childhood or present circumstances.
Underneath that fear lurks
hurt and vulnerability.
If you really want to forgive someone,
look beneath the surface and see what is there.

✳

"Only true understanding can
bring about forgiveness.
And this kind of understanding is possible
when you see the suffering of others."
—THICH NHAT HANH

✳

However much someone deserves your hatred,
hating them will end up making you
the biggest victim of your own hatred.
The deeper the valley of hatred grows,
the more it comes to feel like you are trapped in hell.
Resolve to be mindful of these negative feelings,
even if for no one else's sake but your own.

＊

"Haemin Sunim,
even though I apologized, she still won't forgive me.
Do I have to get down on my knees and beg?"
Things don't get forgiven right away
just because you say you're sorry.
She has suffered a lot because of you,
so it'll take more than a couple apologies
for her to forgive you.
If you are truly sorry, you ought to
apologize sincerely many times.
It's easy to say a few words—too easy, in her eyes,
compared with the pain she has had to endure.

＊

When you look at the situation calmly,
you see that the person who wronged you
behaved badly not only to you,
but also to everyone in a similar position.
His terrible character is obviously to blame.
So don't take personally
what he said or did to you.
The problem is not you. It is him.

✳

When she says hurtful things,
is it really in response to something you did,
or is there another explanation?
If it is the latter, then there is no need to take the blame
for something you have not caused.

✳

If you are stressed out,
maybe it's because your mind is overcrowded
with other people's thoughts and activities.
If this is the case, go on a "media fast" for three days—
forgo your cell phone, TV, and internet.
You will soon be able to listen
to your own body and mind
and return to a state of good health.

✳

If your desk or the floor of your room is messy,
it attracts more mess.
And, of course, it doesn't help you to work efficiently.
When you get home from work and change your clothes,
even if it's irritating, it helps to hang them up in the closet.

＊

Like someone who quits smoking for their health,
my friend said he quit all news for a month.
And he really did stop being distracted and anxious.
Ask yourself whether you truly need to know
the latest news about politics, accidents, and celebrities.
We mindlessly consume it all without thinking.
And, like instant noodles, it provides no nutrients.

＊

When we are alone in a peaceful place,
we experience the stillness of our mind.
It is nourishing and restorative, like medicine, helping us to
recover our center and feel the divinity within us.
A dose of stillness once in a while does a lot of good.

＊

Life's pain is not something to be overcome.
Instead, it calls for gentle love and healing.
The more forcefully we deny it,
or try to forget about it, the stronger it rises up.
Gaze warmly at your pain,
without denying or resisting it.
If you do, you will detect the love
that lies beneath it.

✳

The good heart that prays for the end of others' suffering
ends its own suffering with such prayers.
Send out your blessings to
family, friends, colleagues, strangers on the street.
A saint acts compassionately not because she is a saint.
Rather, her compassionate acts make her a saint.

✳

So you feel terrible today.
But that doesn't mean your whole life is terrible.
Right now you feel drained and worn down.
But you will feel better after a good night's sleep.

✳

The heart's wounds are healed
when we encounter beauty or humor.
When we walk amid the beauty of nature, our thoughts rest.
When we look at beautiful art, our sensibilities are
stimulated.
When we talk with a humorous friend, our mind brightens.
Through beauty and humor, we return
to our original state and become whole again.

＊

I heard the following joke from another monk:
A novice monk asks a senior monk,
"Is it appropriate for a monk to use email?"
The senior monk answers,
"Sure, but only if there are no attachments!"

＊

If you want to kindle firewood,
there needs to be space between the logs.
If you pack the wood too densely,
the fire will not take; the flames need room to breathe.
In the same way, if our lives have no breathing room,
we won't be able to enjoy all the things we have,
no matter how great or precious they are.

＊

When you have somewhere to go,
set out ten minutes early.
Your mind won't be rushed,
and you will be able to enjoy the walk.
Similarly, take an extra five minutes to enjoy a meal.
You will be able to taste the food properly,
and the meal won't sit heavy in your stomach.
A mere five or ten minutes here and there
can dramatically improve your quality of life.

✳

If you own several of the same thing,
keep only the one you like best, and give the others away.
If we have too many possessions,
we do not possess them; they possess us.
A clean space, with everything neat and tidy,
is the greatest luxury, setting our minds at ease.

✳

Choose two or three objects per day
that you haven't used in a while,
and give or throw them away:
food, medicine, and cosmetics
that have passed their use-by date,
clothes you haven't worn in years,
books you've read but won't read again,
appliances that are just taking up space.
If you get rid of them, you don't lose but gain.
Uncluttered space is a source of comfort and relaxation,
and you are left with only the things that make you happy.

"HAEMIN, I AM A LITTLE DEPRESSED"

OVER THE COURSE OF OUR LIVES, most of us go through periods of depression. It would be wonderful if our lives were filled with only joy and happiness, but there is also aging, falling ill, and dying to contend with. It's only to be expected that we will feel depressed at some point, when confronted with the inevitable.

If I look at my own life, depression is like a guest who shows up just when I've managed to forget about him—when my relationships with colleagues were strained by misunderstandings, when my hard work did not pay off, when I got sick but didn't know the cause or how to treat it. I saw no hope of escaping from these circumstances, and depression crawled in.

Since founding a nonprofit organization in Seoul called the School of Broken Hearts, I have had many occasions to meet people like me who experience occasional mild depression. The school offers free support programs for those struggling with cancer, loss of family, divorce, raising a child with a disability, LGBT issues, unemployment, relationship problems, and more. Most participants are not clinically depressed; if they are, we urge them to see a medical doctor right away. But to those experiencing mild depression every once in a while, I have been giving the following advice from the perspective of Buddhist psychology.

WHENEVER FEELINGS OF DEPRESSION have taken hold, I've examined my mind carefully and discovered some striking characteristics about it. First of all, what has triggered my depression and kept feeding it was none other than my own repetitive thoughts. Depending on what kinds of thoughts we have, they have huge bearing on our emotional lives. A positive thought produces a positive feeling, whereas a negative thought leads to a negative feeling. If we don't keep throwing the firewood of depressing thoughts into our mind's furnace, the depressed feeling remains only a visitor, disappearing along with the thought. So if we want to understand feelings of depression, we must first understand the thoughts that give rise to them.

Thoughts are our own individual perspectives on the external and internal situations we call our lives. According to scientists, people have as many as seventeen thousand thoughts in a single day; many thoughts tend to be similar in content, and those that recur most frequently have to do with memories. We become habituated to thinking about the same episodes over and over again. The problem is that for the most part, we are often lost in our thoughts and remain completely unaware of them. Although thoughts are produced by our own minds, they have the power to determine our emotional lives, frequently against our will. Moreover, since thoughts tend to operate on a subconscious level, we cannot easily distinguish between those that reflect objective reality and those that reflect our subjective opinions. This means we are quick to believe that our thoughts are a clear reflection of reality even when this is absolutely not the case.

IN LIGHT OF WHAT WE KNOW about the nature of thoughts, there are three tips I want to offer about how to beat back depression. First, when a depressing thought comes to you, remember that it is only a single, passing cloud in the big sky of your mind. Many psychological problems come about because we confuse our evanescent thoughts with ourselves. But thoughts are only fleeting responses to specific circumstances, which are themselves constantly changing. When we step back and observe a depressing thought, we can see how insignificant it is in the grand scheme of things. And if we leave it alone rather than engage with it, it either disappears on its own or changes shape. We can say to it, "Oh, how interesting! A cloud is passing overhead," and soon it will end up dying out. But if we attach ourselves to the thought and identify with it, rather than perceiving it as separate from ourselves, then we let it linger and end up falling into the swamp of depression.

Second, if your depression is triggered by negative comments about you by people who don't know you very well, you should understand that though it sounds like they're talking about you, their words say more about their own negative psychological state than they do about you. Their comments are based on their own projection of who they imagine you to be. Although you can hope that such people become happier and less mean-spirited, you cannot hold yourself responsible for their negative state of mind, which you have not caused. If you don't give them your attention, they cannot hold so much power over you.

Third, we have to keep in mind that most thoughts are personal opinions based on our limited experience. They are not set in stone but change as the situation does. So if you catch yourself having negative thoughts, rather than thinking too seriously about them, simply turn your attention to the present moment and breathe. It's always helpful to focus on breathing, because breathing always happens in the present. When you feel your breath moving in and out of your body, your mind relaxes, and any tension in your body eases. And when your mind arrives at the here and now, your thoughts naturally stop. In fact, try setting this book down for a moment and breathing deeply for just one minute. Remember that an easy way to release your mind from the trap of negative thoughts and feelings is to focus on the present moment through your breathing.

Now try to feel your breathing.
Breathe deeply, in and out. . . .
Healing begins when
we start to attend to ourselves.

＊

We all experience feelings of depression
at some point in our lives.
When you do, notice that the fuel
for depressed feelings is negative thoughts.
If we keep feeding the feeling with those thoughts,
the feeling grows stronger and stays longer.
Rather than being trapped in negative thoughts,
shift your attention to your body and breathe deeply.
As the mind clears, so will the feeling.

＊

Clouds release their sadness
by crying until they can cry no more.
When they have no tears left to cry,
they feel a great weight has been lifted,
as heavy as all the tears they have shed.
We can release our sadness into the sky within us.
When we feel sad, it's okay to cry like the clouds.

*

When sadness visits you,
don't try to push it away.
Instead, walk right into its center
and embrace your sadness.
After many hours of crying,
you will begin to see
the light at the end of the tunnel.

*

Don't trust your negative thoughts,
especially when times are hard.
When you're in pain, it feels like
the pain will always be with you;
when you fail, it feels like
you'll never pick yourself up again;
when you've experienced loss, it feels like
the wound will never heal.
But nothing lasts forever,
not even your hard times.
You will get better.

*

When you are stressed out by too many thoughts,
pay attention to the object right in front of you.
Really see the object as closely as you can.
What is its color, texture, style, material?
When you focus on something in front of you,
your thoughts naturally stop, because the mind
cannot do two things at once.

*

When difficult emotions
like loneliness, sadness, and fear
well up inside you,
the most courageous thing you can do
is to spend some time with them.
Rather than trying to escape them
by turning on the TV or calling a friend,
sit next to them and look at them quietly.
When you pay attention to them,
they will either change their shape and disappear,
or make you see that they're not that terrifying.

*

Perhaps we interfere in other people's lives
because we are too afraid to face
the emptiness and loneliness in our own.

*

Even the person who looks like he has it all
is living in a hell of his own.
We all face challenges that others can't imagine.
Remember that appearances aren't everything.

*

Often the real cause of depression
is not sadness but anger.
Although you were very angry,
you had to hold your anger in.
And then you felt weak and pathetic
for having been stepped on like a doormat.
Your anger then ended up attacking you
instead of the person who made you angry.
If you are suffering from depression,
consider whether you are suppressing anger.

*

If you think about only your own problems,
they seem big and unique to you,
and you can become depressed.
But if you begin to care about the problems of others,
you realize that yours are neither big nor unique.

*

One way to overcome
feelings of emptiness, irritation, or depression
is to perform a small act of kindness for somebody else.
Try saying to yourself,
"Even though I'm busy,
today I will treat someone else with kindness."
The small gesture expressing that good intention
can become the seed of great change.

Find happiness not in financial or business success,
but by spending time with friends and loved ones.
When you've achieved your professional goals,
you end up setting new and higher ones,
making you feel you still don't have enough.
Happiness then becomes a mirage, forever out of reach.
But time spent with friends brings us happiness
not in the future but in the here and now.
Having close friends whom we can share
both the good and bad times with
is one of the sure ways to happiness.

＊

When your life feels empty and mildly depressing,
see if you can do one of the following.
1. Learn something new: It could be anything—
a musical instrument, a craft, a sport, a foreign language.
2. Spend two to three hours a week volunteering:
You will feel good for doing something meaningful.
3. Invite friends for lunch:
When we feel connected, we feel less depressed and lonely.
4. Meditate on the truth of impermanence in this world:
It is natural for things to change.
Willingly accept that change.

*

Imagine that you've achieved everything you had hoped for.
You found a good job, a loving spouse,
and the house of your dreams.
You got promoted, and your children
are doing well in school.
You survived illness, and you have ample savings.
You can finally relax and stop worrying, right?
But how about two or three months from now?
You will inevitably find new things to worry about.
Even if our circumstances change for the better,
if our habit of mind hasn't changed,
we will wind up finding new things to be unhappy about.

*

Even if we are born in heaven,
some people will still find fault.
They will say that heaven is too perfect and too nice.

*

"I think everybody should get rich and famous
and do everything they ever dreamed of
so they can see that it's not the answer."
—JIM CARREY, VIA TWITTER

＊

I went to a smart new café in my neighborhood.
I wanted to order a delicious-looking slice of cake,
but when I heard how expensive it was,
I just ordered some tea.
But I had that cake in my mind for the rest of the day.
After two days, I still couldn't get it out of my mind,
so I went back to the café, bought a slice, and ate it.
It was delicious, but not extraordinarily delicious.
This must be the kind of feeling people have
after winning the Nobel Prize or becoming president.

＊

We sometimes find it difficult
to control our emotions.
At such times, take some quiet time alone.
Go for a walk on your own, watch a great film,
read a new book, or do some meditation.
Give the suppressed emotion space
until it can breathe easily.

*

In Thich Nhat Hanh's Plum Village,
one day a week is a lazy day,
when people greet each other by asking,
"How lazy are you today?"
Give yourself the gift of a lazy day one day a week.
Make friends with the blue sky or the cool breeze.

*

There are times when all you want to do
is lie on the couch and watch TV.
It's about time you gave your hardworking mind
a moment to relax.
You can't be productive all the time.

*

When the world knocks you down,
get back up and keep on walking.
Even if the pain makes you cry,
even if you want to die of embarrassment,
just carry on.
As you keep on walking, things will get better.
As you keep on walking, things will be forgotten.
You are a brave soul, choosing to grow through pain.
I am rooting for you!

✳

"Suffering is a door
that opens onto a new world."
—CARDINAL KIM SOU-HWAN

There is always a gap
between what you know and how you act.
Just because you have read an inspiring book
or received a great lesson from a spiritual teacher,
it doesn't mean your life will change instantly.
Only when you put your new knowledge into
action,
slowly and with a lot of effort,
will change begin to come.
In Buddhism, too, the experience of
enlightenment
is followed by a lifetime work of bodhisattva,
helping all living beings in this world
to close this gap.

Chapter Seven

ENLIGHTENMENT

The true nature of our mind is like the sky.
Our thoughts are like clouds,
our emotions like lightning,
and the sky accepts them all equally,
watching as they shift and move across it.
The weather of thoughts and emotions rises
    and passes away,
but the sky remains the same—clear,
    luminous, open.

THE MIND'S TRUE HOME

AFTER TWO DAYS OF SUMMER rain speeding the advance of autumn, the sky finally cleared, poking its blue face out from between the clouds. With the blue sky for a backdrop, the trees' leaves danced excitedly in the wind, like red and yellow waving hands. For me, early autumn is always a time to go on a meditation retreat. I usually go to a mountain monastery in Korea, but this year I went to Plum Village, the Buddhist community near Bordeaux, France, established by the Vietnamese monk Thich Nhat Hanh. When Thich Nhat Hanh visited Korea in 2013 along with his disciples, I served as his interpreter for his public talks and formed a precious relationship with him. I had always wanted to see for myself how his wonderful teachings were put into practice in Plum Village, so when the opportunity presented itself to visit, I seized it.

At the time of the Vietnam War, Thich Nhat Hanh led

the antiwar movement inside and outside of Vietnam. Seeing his efforts, Martin Luther King Jr. was greatly moved and nominated him for the Nobel Peace Prize. After the war, Thich Nhat Hanh was unable to return to Vietnam, so he settled in France, where he started a small Buddhist community together with those who came to seek his teachings. As time passed, what had originally been a small commune attracted ever larger numbers of visiting practitioners. Unfortunately, Thich Nhat Hanh's health has been in decline since 2014, and he has been unable to give public teachings. In spite of this, many people from all over the world still visit Plum Village in order to practice mindfulness meditation.

When I first arrived at Plum Village, I was immediately struck by how slowly everybody walked. It was a marked contrast with daily life in towns and cities, where everybody is always in a rush. The monks and lay practitioners of Plum Village walk slowly not only to deepen their mindfulness but also to enjoy the act of walking itself. And I discovered that it wasn't just walking; they also eat very slowly, a mouthful at a time, quietly savoring the meal. No matter what delicacy we might have in front of us, if our mind wanders while we are eating, then we won't be able to taste a thing. But if our mind is fully alert, even a mouthful of tea can taste like nothing we have ever experienced before.

THICH NHAT HANH'S MOST IMPORTANT teaching is that the mind must be fully present in the here and now, including while we walk and eat. Rather than getting caught up in its own thoughts, mulling over past memories or future worries, the mind stays in the present moment because the place of enlightenment that practitioners seek is in the here and now, the mind's true home. When our mind is fully present, it naturally becomes calm and centered, without many distracting thoughts, allowing us to enjoy our lives fully and focus on what we do—whether it is having a conversation with our friends, cooking a meal for family, or cleaning floors.

Thich Nhat Hanh also teaches that we should be mindful of our breathing, as it is an important bridge between body and mind. If our breathing is calm, our mind will be calm, and if our breathing is agitated, our mind will be agitated. The same goes the other way around: Frantic minds make for frantic breathing, and peaceful minds produce peaceful breathing. In addition, breathing always happens in the here and now and thus anchors our mind in the present. As we breathe more calmly and deeply, the mind follows suit, savoring deep and peaceful silence.

AS MY PRACTICE OF MINDFUL breathing deepens, the door of wisdom begins to open. People typically equate the mind with thoughts, as if thoughts are the only things there. However, once experiencing the peaceful silence that lies in the gap between one thought and the next, I see how a thought appears from that silence and also disappears into it by itself. Consequently, I don't attach too much importance to each thought but pay more attention to the quiet space in between thoughts. The space of silence then gradually expands, and I begin to feel that even a good thought is not as pleasant as the peaceful silence.

Eventually I come to realize that this peaceful silence exists not only inside my body, but outside it as well, as it is impossible to pinpoint precisely where the silence begins and ends. The conceptual division between the self and the world collapses, and I come to realize that the silence is the mind's unshakable true nature as well as the unmanifested ground of the universe before its creation. I finally come to understand the Zen proverb "There is no difference whatsoever among the mind, the world, and the Buddha."

WHILE THE SKY IS DYED ORANGE and red by the sunset, a monk solemnly rings the evening bell. The sound echoes reverently throughout the grounds of Plum Village. It is accompanied by the sounds of gentle footsteps, as people make their way toward the meditation hall. Seeing all this, my heart blooms into a flower of gratitude and contentment.

✳

When you eat your next meal, try closing your eyes.
We tend to rely on sight far more than on the other senses.
If you close your eyes and slowly savor the taste,
a whole new world will open up to you.

✳

Five ways to clear your thoughts and find peace in the
present:
Look at beautiful scenery, and smile.
Close your eyes and breathe deeply ten times.
Listen to music with your eyes closed.
Enjoy walking without a destination in mind.
Shift your attention to your body, focusing on how your
shoulders and back feel.

✳

When you are lost in thought,
you might not see what is right in front of you.
But if you concentrate on what is right in front of you,
you will be able to pause your thoughts.
Rather than struggling to stop your thoughts,
simply look at what is in front of you.
This brings the mind to the present.

＊

Breathing is an incredible time machine,
bringing our minds
from thoughts of the past or the future
back to the present moment.

＊

When a baseball player hits a home run,
after passing first, second, and third base,
he returns to home base, where he started.
When we begin our spiritual journey,
we leave home in search of something wonderful,
only to realize that what we long sought
has been inside us all along.

＊

When your mind focuses on your breathing,
becoming fully alert and free of idle thoughts,
you suddenly realize
that the peace and contentment in your mind
is more precious than anything you can buy.

*

If you get up very early in the morning,
with your house dark and the world quiet,
try listening to the sound of silence.
Feel both its emptiness and fullness.
Silence is tranquil, immaculate, and comforting.
It doesn't demand anything from you.
No matter where you are,
the feeling of calm wholeness is available
to anyone who just listens quietly.

*

Don't assume that a still mind is boring.
Inside the stillness
hides the utmost peace and contentment.
If the mind is fully alert to that stillness,
it will also discover its true nature,
indestructible even after death.

*

Your true nature is not something
you can obtain by searching for it.
It will reveal itself to you
when the mind grows quiet.

When the sky is empty of clouds,
we can see its blue depths.
And when the mind is empty of thoughts,
we can feel its true nature.

✳

"Silence is deep as Eternity;
speech is shallow as Time."
—THOMAS CARLYLE

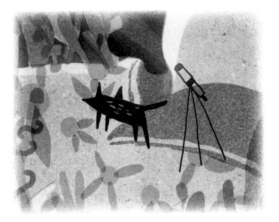

＊

Thoughts and emotions surface and recede inside the mind.
But what is it that registers their coming and going?
Is it another thought, or something else?
If it is another thought, then that thought
must be known as well.
And then what is that which knows *that* thought?
If you look deeply, it is not another thought.
It is the inner silence that knows.
That formless and immaculate silence is your true nature.

＊

The mind is like a mirror,
which nothing can ever mark or mar.
In the mind's mirror, jealousy, hatred, and greed
can be reflected as fleeting images.
But these are only reflections on the mirror's surface;
the mirror itself is not marked by them.
Do not see yourself in mere reflections,
mistakenly imagining that they are yourself.

*

When thoughts or emotions arise,
do not attach the word "I" to them,
assuming that they are
"my thoughts" or "my emotions."
They usually linger only briefly.
If you keep claiming them as yours,
you will only obstruct their natural flow
and mistakenly identify with them.

*

Thoughts are passing clouds,
appearing in response to an array of factors
beyond your control.
Clinging to a particular negative thought
can even lead to depression.
Be careful not to get caught up in your thoughts.

*

"True freedom is
freedom from the known."
—JIDDU KRISHNAMURTI

＊

Any object that can be observed is not your true nature.
For example, a cup, tree, or building can be observed,
which means they are not you, the observer, but objects.
In the same way, thoughts and emotions can be observed,
but you still remain even after they disappear into silence.
The main reason we suffer is because we mistakenly
equate objects with the observer.

＊

"You find peace not by rearranging
the circumstances of your life,
but by realizing who you are
at the deepest level."
—ECKHART TOLLE

＊

Our true self can never be lost,
even for a single moment.
Just like the present can never be lost—
it is always here and now,
whether or not we pay attention to it.

＊

"True freedom
is being without anxiety about imperfection."
—ZEN MASTER SENGCHAN

Your life is difficult
not because the past is holding you back,
but because you keep thinking about the past
and lingering there.
Rather than haggling with your past,
let it be, so that it can flow like a river.
Your true self is not the river of memory
but the one who stands beside the river,
quietly observing its flow.

MY SPIRITUAL JOURNEY

When I was in high school, I didn't know much about Buddhism, just enough to look forward to Buddha's birthday every May. I liked having a day off from school at that time of year, when the weather was usually nice. I also enjoyed the sight of the colorful paper lanterns decorating the streets of Seoul. When I walked through those lantern-lit streets at dusk, it was so beautiful that I could almost forget about school or my uncertainty about the future. At this time of year I would often visit Doseon Temple on Mount Bukhan, which was not far from my home. While passing beneath the colorful lanterns and listening on my Walkman to my favorite musicians, like George Winston, Enya, or Simon and Garfunkel, I became peaceful and at ease.

On weekends, there was one thing I especially enjoyed doing: hanging out with American missionaries. They were in their early twenties, only three or four years older than I was, so it was easy to become friends with them. We would play sports and card games, and teach each other about our culture and language. Our interactions also strengthened my interest in religion and led me to explore questions like "Why are we born, and what becomes of us after we die?" "Who am I?" and "Why is the world so full of inequality and suffering?" I liked being able to discuss these questions in English, perhaps because they were the kinds of questions I wasn't allowed to ask in school.

When Buddha's birthday came around, I persuaded my missionary friends that, since they had come to Korea, they should get to know a traditional Korean religion. At the time I wouldn't have felt qualified to call myself a Buddhist; I simply enjoyed introducing my foreign friends to a tradition that was an important part of Korean history and culture. Perhaps because they agreed about the value of understanding another religion, or because they just wanted to venture outside the city, late one afternoon, when the lanterns were at their most striking, my missionary friends headed with me up Mount Bukhan to Doseon Temple.

Upon arriving, we admired the traditional buildings and grounds. Then my missionary friends started asking me questions. For instance, seeing the dignified and yet frightening faces of the Four Heavenly Guardian Kings at the entrance to the temple grounds, they asked, "Why do Buddhists worship gods who look like devils?"; pointing to the people bowing before the carved stone Buddha statue, they asked, "Why are they bowing to a stone Buddha? Isn't that idol worship?" I couldn't muster even a lame explanation, never mind an informed one, not knowing enough at the time to be able to answer that, just as in Christianity the archangels Gabriel and Michael serve the will of God and protect the faithful, Buddhism has its own otherworldly beings, like the Four Heavenly Guardian Kings, who protect the teachings of the Buddha and the Buddha's followers. When I was in high school, I also misunderstood what the Buddha statue represented, simply assuming that the Buddha was like a deity with great powers, granting people's prayers if they worshipped him sincerely. Thinking back now, I'm struck by how ignorant I was.

IN COLLEGE I STARTED TO LEARN about Buddhism and read several Buddhist texts as part of my major in religious studies. One of them was the Diamond Sutra, an important Mahayana scripture, which taught me that "the true Buddha has no form and, therefore, cannot be seen with the eyes." In other words, the Buddha signifies the enlightened mind and has no particular shape or human form. All living beings are said to have "Buddha nature" or "true nature," and once we become enlightened, we are no different from the Buddha. Although we bow before an image of the Buddha, what we are ultimately expressing reverence to is the mind's true nature, which exists formlessly in the present moment.

Later, while I was training to become a monk, I studied Zen Buddhist texts such as the Recorded Sayings of Zen

Masters, which contains the sayings of ancient teachers, pointing readers directly to the enlightened mind. For example: "If the stone Buddha seems sacred to us, is it because of the inherent sacredness in the image or because of our minds seeing it as sacred?" Even if two people look at the same stone Buddha, it might feel sacred to one and not at all to the other. Does true sacredness dwell in the stone that bears the Buddha's image, or in the mind, which knows sacredness?

The opportunity arose for me to directly experience things that I had so far experienced only through academic study. It was the intensive Zen meditation retreat at Beomeo Monastery, led by the great Zen master Subul. I resolved to do my best and just follow what the master was teaching. And, luckily, I was able to experience various stages of meditation that I had only read about. All thoughts completely fell away, and I was finally able to experience the first taste of the enlightened mind.

It is difficult to describe the enlightened mind in words, but it is free of thoughts and feels silent, peaceful, transparent, free, alive, weightless, limitless, and indestructible. It exists in its fullness, not only inside the body but also in the outside universe, as one seamless, undivided consciousness. It also has the quality of knowing. Every time we know something, it is with this quality of the enlightened mind; it is not something mystical or out of this world. The enlightened mind exists so closely to us that we have overlooked it all of our lives. Like the empty sky, which allows clouds, lightning,

and rain; like silence, which becomes the background to all music and sound; like a mirror, which reflects everything in the world as it is; like a loving mother, who always watches her child, the enlightened mind exists to everyone at all times, including right now.

AFTER THIS SERIES OF EXPERIENCES, my life changed unexpectedly. Somehow I began to be known in South Korea through my writings. There were many areas in which I was lacking, and with people seeking me out and asking me to teach them about Buddhism when there was still a lot I needed to practice, I felt embarrassed. I decided to deepen my meditation before it was too late and went to Bongam Monastery. I was happy to be back and to spend time with monastic brothers and with Zen master Jeokmyeong, who had dedicated his whole life to study and meditation.

Zen master Jeokmyeong said to me: "Even if you arrive at just the first stage of the bodhisattva path, you will have enough wisdom to comprehend most Buddhist texts without any problem. But the reason you still need to cultivate nine more stages in order to reach the tenth is because there is a gap between what you know and how you act. Only when everyday people on the street see your compassionate and wise actions and declare, 'You're like a living Buddha!' can you believe that you have closed the gap."

THE HARDEST THING IN THE WORLD is putting what you know into practice, and making sure your actions do not contradict your words. Looking at myself, the gap between the two still seems very wide. But regardless of the circumstances I find myself in, I would like to stay mindful and continue to cultivate a compassionate heart. Though it may take a long time, I resolve to reduce the gap as much as I can in this lifetime. As I write this, the Buddha's birthday is only a week away, and the colorful lanterns hanging in the streets of Seoul are as beautiful now as they were when I was a schoolboy.

*

Your body is older,
but your mind may not feel that way.
It is because the mind knows no age.
It exists in the eternal now.

*

In contrast to the boundless universe,
does your mind feel small, locked inside your body?
The truth is that your mind isn't locked inside.
The reason the mind can know the universe
is that it is as big as the universe.
If your mind exists only inside your body,
your knowledge should be limited to
what goes on inside your body.
But you know things outside your body.
Whenever knowing occurs, your mind is there, too.

*

The knowing mind
and the space in which knowing occurs
are one and the same.

*

When it is rainy and cold outside,
we naturally seek our warm and cozy home.
When we are beset with difficulties,
we naturally become more alert and mindful.
When things are going well, we don't meditate much.
Difficulties are blessings in disguise to foster mindfulness.

*

Mindfulness isn't something that
has to be done in a special place.
That uncomfortable point where
your mind rubs up against the world
is the best place to practice mindfulness.

*

There is no better teacher than the people you dislike
as they get you to examine your mind more deeply.
As Zen master Seongcheol said,
"The greatest learning opportunity is when
you get blamed for what you have not caused."

✳

Overcoming the wounds or trauma of the past
through spiritual practice alone is not easy.
Physical exercise—like hiking, swimming, or yoga—
combined with psychological counseling
can be more effective than spiritual practice alone.
If you go straight into meditation
with your psychological wounds left untreated,
your memory of the pain
may hold you back from making progress.

✳

Don't overtax your body and mind in the hope of
accelerating the progress of your meditation.
Get enough sleep, eat a balanced diet, exercise regularly.
Avoid straining your body by sitting for too long.
Your progress will be quicker when your body and mind
are in equilibrium and at ease.

✳

You make great efforts to attain enlightenment,
only to realize that it has always been
in your hand from the beginning.
You try hard to obtain God's love,
only to realize that there has never been
a single moment when God has not loved you.

＊

When we are enlightened,
we realize that the whole universe is also enlightened.
The Buddha helps sentient beings everywhere,
all the while knowing perfectly well that
everyone is Buddha, and everything is in his mind.

＊

The doors to the enlightened mind are reached through the
following:
love, silence, acceptance, the present moment,
the feeling of aliveness, open awareness,
the mind with no thought, complete surrender.

＊

Becoming enlightened does not mean
you immediately become perfect.
Even after attaining enlightenment,
you must work to align your new awareness
with your actions, particularly in human relationships.
Learn all the mundane knowledge in the world
but use it for a higher purpose.
Enlightenment is not the end but the beginning.

*

The truly enlightened teacher does not ask his students
to follow him exclusively.
If there are other great teachers,
he encourages his students to learn from them, too.
His primary concern is his students' spiritual growth,
not the maintenance of his power.
If the teacher is worshipped like a god,
and he seems to enjoy it, be wary.

*

If there is only intelligence and no sensitivity,
you won't know how to empathize
when faced with someone's suffering.
If there is only sensitivity but no spirituality,
you may lose hope and fall into despair
when faced with your own suffering.
If there is only spirituality and no intelligence,
you may join a cult and come to suffer.

224

*

Do not be easily taken in by someone
who proclaims their own enlightenment.
Enlightenment is the absence of the "I."
According to the Heart Sutra,
you are liberated when you realize
that there is nothing to be attained.
Then who is this "I" attaining enlightenment?

*

"Strictly speaking, there are no enlightened people,
there is only enlightened activity."
—ZEN MASTER SHUNRYU SUZUKI

*

According to the sayings of a Zen master
from the Song dynasty:
"When it snows, three kinds of monks can be
seen in the temple.
The first kind goes into the meditation hall and sits.
The second kind debates the nature of enlightenment.
The third kind chats about today's meals.
Who am I, who likes all three?"

＊

When you feel, "I can't be bothered to do anything today,"
all your mindfulness goes out the window.
Be careful not to succumb to inertia.

＊

There is one way to tell whether you need
to keep doing your meditation practice or not.
Is there still something you need to ask a teacher?
If so, then you still have a little further to go.

＊

Being enlightened to your true nature means
experiencing firsthand what you have known for a long time
but have not yet managed to experience.
We have yet to attain enlightenment
not because we don't know the path,
but because we have not yet experienced
what we already know.
The day you become enlightened,
you will understand why the great teachers
have said what they have said.

✳

"When the mind is at rest,
I see the moon rising and the wind blowing gently.
Then I realize that the world is not necessarily
an ocean of suffering."
— *CAIGENTAN*

Chapter Eight

ACCEPTANCE

If you're sad, it's okay to acknowledge your sadness.
If you have pain that leaves you at a loss,
it's okay to talk about your pain.
The reason we have difficulties
is that we are unable to accept
the things that cannot be changed.
Let them be and see what happens.

THE ART OF LETTING GO

"LET IT GO" is advice we often hear, but it's difficult to know how to put it into practice. I've met many people whose distress stems from their inability to move on from setbacks or let impossible dreams go. For example, if someone irritates us, we would like to forget the incident as soon as we can and move on. But even though we try to let it go, we end up recalling the incident and upsetting ourselves again. Then there are times when we are on the cusp of achieving a major goal we have been working toward, only to fall at the final hurdle. When we attempt to identify a new goal, the memories, regrets, and frustrations come back and torment us, leaving us unable to focus on anything.

"Let it go" is actually another way of expressing "Accept it fully." It does not mean that the painful memory will somehow disappear. We might wish to erase the past like we wipe chalk off a blackboard, but it's simply not possible. And the more we struggle to forget, the more we give strength to the memory and get attached to it. But there is one very important thing to remember: What causes us such distress is not the memory itself but the emotions that surround it—like regret, disappointment, anger, and frustration.

This might seem subtle, but it is important to distinguish the memory from its emotions. A disappointing or hurtful situation from ten years ago doesn't cause us the same distress now as it did then. This is because the emotions surrounding the memory have been either extinguished or alleviated. The memory itself is not the problem—it's still there; it's the emotions connected to the memory that are the problem. And so there's no need to suppress the memory or try to get rid of it, which is nearly impossible anyway.

So what should we do if we want to let something go? The answer is to accept ourselves just as we are. If we accept the struggling self, our state of mind will soon undergo a change, though it will be subtle at first. When we regard our difficult emotions as a problem, and try to overcome them, we only struggle more. In contrast, when we accept them, strangely enough our mind stops struggling, and grows suddenly quiet. And when that happens, it becomes possible to leave our emotions behind and look at them warmly from the outside. Rather than trying to change or control difficult emotions from the inside, allow them to be there, and your mind will rest. When this happens, you can more easily detach yourself and look at your emotions calmly, as though they belong to someone else.

When our mind is quiet and we look at our emotions from the outside, something unexpected happens: We sense the loving presence of our inner silence, watching those emotions with composure. If you are religious, the inner silence may feel like the presence of God or another transcendental being. We thought we were struggling alone in the world, but in the stillness we sense "the one" who is always with us, who looks at our mind with compassion. When things get especially difficult, some of us even purportedly hear words coming from the silence or from God, saying, "Things are so hard for you right now, but you will be okay no matter what."

When we arrive at this point, we can sense some distance between our difficult emotions and ourselves, and no longer identify ourselves with these emotions. Then we can allow them to exist, since they don't bother us as much. Previously they were overpowering, because we felt they were taking up all the space within the small confines of our mind. But then the walls crumble, and those same emotions are now in a warm, tranquil, wide-open space, where we can see them clearly. Even though the emotions haven't disappeared, they don't seem like such a huge problem anymore. You have neither avoided nor altered them, but with gradual acceptance of them comes a corresponding peace.

DURING THE TIMES in your life when your inability to let something go leaves you feeling distressed, please don't try to fight it. Instead, allow it to be there, and then observe it without words. Your mind will soon become quiet and spacious, making it easier to live with your negative feelings. Then you may even see the eyes of compassion inside you that look on your inner wound with love. As this happens, your mind will realize that you are not the wound, but the deep silence that knows the wound.

*

When you feel bad, don't struggle with the feeling.
If you struggle to control it, you can make it worse.
However hard you might wish your feelings away,
they will stay for as long as they need to.
When you allow them to be there and watch them,
they usually leave earlier than you expected.

*

Emotions are like uninvited guests.
They come whenever they want to,
and leave once you acknowledge their presence.
Although emotions are born inside of you,
don't assume that they belong to you.
That is why they rarely listen to you.

*

The moment we allow ourselves to be,
we finally feel at peace with ourselves.
Remember that we can only be ourselves.
When we accept ourselves,
others begin to accept us, too.

＊

If you fully accept your difficult emotion,
be it loneliness, anger, sadness, or frustration,
you will derive strength from that acceptance.
After acknowledging the truth of the situation,
new wisdom and courage will manifest in you
so you can face the next stage.

＊

You can't let your obsession go
just by thinking to yourself, "I need to drop this."
Only when you see that obsession brings
suffering in the end, will you be able to drop it.
You were rushing to lick honey off a razor's edge.

＊

If you insist that someone change their life,
it could be because you are not happy with your own.

*

Do you often say to your loved one,
"If you love me, can't you change for me?"
That is not love.
Love's true face is acceptance and freedom,
not restriction and control.

*

If you've often had to deny yourself what you want,
you may unwittingly deny the wishes of others,
feeling that people should live their lives like you live yours.
If you stop denying yourself,
it will become easier to accept others as they are.

*

Until you started thinking something was a problem,
it hadn't really bothered you much, had it?
Labeling something a problem is often what makes it one.

There are people who say,
"They're the problem, not me.
Why do they keep telling me to change?"
But think about it for a moment.
If you asked them what the problem was,
how would they answer?
Wouldn't they also say that it's not themselves but you?
If neither of you backs down,
you won't get anywhere.
And it's much quicker to change your own behavior
than to convince someone else to change theirs.
If you give a little ground, they'll probably do so, too.

✳

When you're upset, remember the words of Dale Carnegie:
"Let's not allow ourselves to be upset
by small things we should despise and forget."
When something upsets you,
recall something upsetting from a year ago.
Does it still bother you?
You probably can't even remember it all that well, right?

*

There are times in our lives when we just want to give up.
Even though it's hard, hold on.
When you feel you absolutely can't take any more,
be patient for just a little while longer.
If you throw in the towel,
everything you've built will be lost,
and you will regret it forever.
Persevering even when things are difficult
reveals your true character.

*

In many things in life, the good is mixed with the bad.
If you throw away the whole thing
because you dislike the bad part,
you'll also throw away much that is good.

*

When someone is praised greatly,
two beats later the criticisms start.

＊

However happy or healthy we manage to be,
it seems nothing can ever be perfect.
If we come into money,
we quarrel over money with our family.
If we obtain a position of power,
our friends try to benefit.
If we succeed at work,
we soon have enemies, jealous of our success.
Learn to accept that such is the way of the world.

＊

When the winter wind blows and the temperature drops,
going outside becomes unpleasant.
But the same cold wind
makes the air pure and clear.
Even things that initially look bad
contain something good, if only we look closely.

＊

"The secret to a happy life
is not chasing after a better job
but learning to enjoy the job you have."
—HYEGWANG SUNIM

＊

People start out trying to achieve success
as the world defines it,
but as they get older,
they begin to enlarge their idea of success.
It is the law of nature that what goes up must come down,
and so people gradually train their sights
away from worldly success and on happiness
in learning, volunteer work, friendships,
and spiritual practice.

＊

Even if you have everything you've ever wanted,
you won't be happy if you're always striving
for more or better.
Happiness comes when our hearts are peaceful and content,
and when we learn to appreciate what we already have.

When you finally achieve something you've wanted
for a long time,
it seems like you'll be happy forever.
But that's not how things go.
After feeling happy and proud for a while,
waves of despondency come flooding in,
and success gives way to a backlash you never anticipated.
Instead of postponing your happiness
until you've achieved your goal,
live a little and enjoy the moment.
Life is passing you by while you are waiting.

We don't become wise by thinking more.
When our mind becomes relaxed and open,
we suddenly have a brilliant new idea.
Trust the wisdom that exists in silence,
and rest your hardworking mind for a while.

LESSONS FROM
LIFE'S LOW POINT

Early last year I was contacted by Shin-soo Choo, a Major League Baseball player for the Texas Rangers. He had read my first book, *The Things You Can See Only When You Slow Down*, and wanted to meet me. Since then, we have formed a close bond, exchanging occasional messages and phone calls. If he had a game in New York, sometimes I would go to cheer him on. In the first half of the year, his batting score wasn't as high as it had been, so he asked me how he might try to get out of his slump. I worried about him, struggling alone in a foreign country like I did, as if he were my younger brother. He was under enormous pressure to help his team win games and live up to the fans' expectations. When I told him what he might consider doing, he said he'd already tried everything he could think of, including my suggestions, but had been unable to find the exact cause of the slump. All of this was weighing heavily on him.

EACH OF US WILL EXPERIENCE something similar in our lives—a situation in which nothing seems to improve, despite our best efforts. I'd recently had a similar experience myself, related to my health. After suffering from a severe cold the previous winter, most of the symptoms had disappeared, but the pain in my throat still lingered. I gargled with salt water and took various medications prescribed by my doctor, including antibiotics, but nothing seemed to help. After several months of this, I even had a CT scan and acupuncture, but the pain still didn't go away, and no one could say exactly why.

Many people who ask me questions via social media or after a public talk find themselves in similar circumstances. When your grades don't improve even though you study hard; when you've spent months putting all your efforts into your business but it doesn't take off; when you've made efforts to improve your relationships at home and at work but nothing changes; when you've done everything the doctor recommended but your illness persists—at such times it's inevitable that we become frustrated and depressed.

We may try going to church, temple, mosque, or synagogue, to pray for help and ask advice, but this doesn't result in the quick fix we were hoping for. When advice like "Just do your best and things will turn out fine" no longer brings us comfort, what should we do?

First, we need to take a step back and get a broader

perspective. There are times when the sea is rough, and other times when it's smooth. There are days when the sun shines bright, and days of torrential rain. Why do we consider good weather to be the norm that bad weather disrupts? Why should the sun always shine on us? The bumpy patch you're on is part of a longer road; we have to learn to take the rough with the smooth, and see both as equal parts of our lives. When we take a broader view, the present slump can be seen as the trough of a wave, which sinks down to gather the energy it needs in order to rise again. It's thanks to these low points that, when we're again riding the crest of the wave, we're able to be humble rather than arrogant, and to have the wisdom not to get carried away.

It is also important to make setbacks an opportunity for cultivating compassion. When our life is progressing smoothly, it's easy to credit our efforts and talent. When we see someone who's not doing as well as we are, in their work or in their relationships, we naturally assume it's at least partly their own fault. If their relationships aren't going well, we think it must be due to some flaw in their character; if they can't get a promotion, it's easy to think it must be because they don't work hard enough.

But the world is like a great web, where everything is connected to everything else, no matter how far apart; so how can anything be due solely to one person's shortcomings? Isn't it possible that some problems can't be solved even with the greatest determination; that people's given situation or background makes some things inherently harder for them than for others? Your will isn't enough to turn your circumstances around; isn't it possible that other people's efforts were no less than yours, yet they, too, were unable to solve their problems? Try making your own slump an opportunity to be more compassionate toward others who are also struggling.

Finally, know that your continuous and accumulated efforts will eventually help to turn your circumstances around. The pitcher Chan Ho Park, the first Korean-born Major League Baseball player, once told me something that sums this up: Whether you are in a slump or riding high, whether fans are cheering or heckling, the only thing you can control is the ball you are about to throw. And though no single ball can do much on its own, taken together, all the balls you throw are enough to bring about a big change.

Your efforts, however small, are never in vain. Even the most vicious storm runs its course eventually; as long as you hold on and don't give up, you'll be able to see the sun come out again. Right now, in the middle of writing this essay, I hear that Shin-soo Choo is on a winning streak. We can do it, all of us!

＊

In the quilt of life,
praise and criticism, pleasure and pain,
winning and losing, joy and sadness
are woven together as one.
Even when we endure criticism or experience loss,
we should become mindful and accept it
with as much humility and grace as we can muster.

＊

Even though it seems like the night will go on forever,
at a certain point the days start getting longer.
Even though it seems suffering will continue without end,
at a certain point it will ease up, or we will learn to accept it.
Meanwhile, we will learn a valuable lesson
from that suffering.
Nothing in this world lasts forever, not even our suffering.

＊

If life were free of adversity,
we wouldn't have many opportunities to grow.
It's in struggling to solve the challenges that life throws at us
that our talents are honed and our endurance builds.

*

Difficulties on the journey of life
prompt us to reexamine our lives
and think of those who are experiencing similar ones,
and so they become a foundation for cultivating compassion.
May the difficulties you are currently experiencing
lead to wisdom and compassion!

*

"Even if someone I helped in the past,
or I expected greatness from, causes me grave harm,
may I consider him my greatest teacher."
—His Holiness the Dalai Lama

*

When seen up close,
we all appear full of problems and inconsistencies.
Our actions often contradict our words.
Depending on whom we are speaking to,
we change our story or profess different values.
We are nice to strangers but not to our family.
The first step to maturity
is becoming aware through introspection
of our own shortcomings.

*

Spiritual maturity
involves facing the most disagreeable parts of yourself
and acknowledging their existence.
Once you accept the selfish, greedy,
and even violent sides of yourself,
you will be able to understand others
and forgive their flaws.

*

The more we mature,
the more we see how much others have contributed
to those successes we have called our own.
When we realize how much we owe to others
and express our deep and sincere gratitude,
the next success will follow.

*

The way to avoid becoming servile before others
who have power, fame, or money
is to be happy with your life.
If there is nothing you need from those people,
you can be confident and dignified with whomever you meet.
When you want something from them, you become servile.

*

The opposite of greed is not abstinence
but knowing how to be content.

*

The voice that criticizes and berates me
is much louder than the one that cheers me on.
When times are tough,
that cheering voice can get drowned out.
But keep listening.
After your critics have moved on to criticize someone else,
you will start to hear those who have stayed behind,
steadily cheering you on.

*

If there are nine good things and one bad thing in our lives,
we'll expend more energy focusing on the one bad thing
than on all that good.
This is a habit left over from primitive times,
when our ancestors needed to be
constantly on the lookout for danger.
If you discover yourself focusing on the bad, tell yourself:
"It's not the prehistoric era anymore.
Worry about bad things when they happen, not before."

＊

One of our deepest fears
is that when we show ourselves as we are,
we will be rejected.
We find it hard to open the door of our heart
even to our closest friends.
Because we carry that burden alone,
it can't help but weigh us down.
When someone opens the door to their heart
and shows themselves as they are,
do not judge them; warmly accept them.
None of us is perfect.

＊

Unless there's a real emergency,
backseat drivers ought to keep quiet.
Everyone has their own way of driving.
If you leave the driving to the driver
and talk about something interesting
until you reach your destination,
everyone will be happy!

*

People often think
that their way of doing things is the right way.
If they see something being done in a way
that is not their own,
they jump in to tell others they're doing it wrong.
But other people's ways are not wrong,
only unfamiliar to you.
Try doing something in a way
that is different from your way.
A new world will open up to you.

*

When somebody annoys you,
recognize that you feel annoyed because
they didn't do something the way you wanted it done.
They may have their own reason
for doing something their way,
which you should not disregard
and try to replace with your own.
If you think about it from their perspective,
you're the one causing the problem.

＊

We suffer as we put off
the things we ought to finish today.
Pick a specific time today
when you will do whatever you've been putting off,
and when the time comes,
don't make excuses, don't get distracted—
just do it.

＊

If you're not sure whether to do something,
ask yourself whether it will weigh heavily on you
if you don't do it.
If it will, then best just to do it.
Otherwise, you will spend more time agonizing over excuses.

＊

If I come across a book I want to read, I just buy it.
I don't have to read it right away;
as long as it's there on my shelf,
I will get to it at some point.
Even if it's a doorstop of a novel,
or a complex work of philosophy,
the time will come when I will be able to enjoy it.

＊

Abruptly asking a monk to give you a meditation lesson
is like asking a comedian to make you laugh on the spot.
Nevertheless, I should accept the request
and have ready several short lessons for such occasions.

＊

"When flowers wilt,
when the sun sets,
when a person's life ends,
even in our deep sadness
we learn the wisdom
to understand and accept life
and learn the humility
to forgive others and ourselves."
—Sister Claudia Lee Hae-in, from "A Small Prayer"

*

I pray that my humble words can become
a small flame of solace steadily burning in your heart.
May they become a friendly smile in this harsh world,
and a warm hug to those in agony and pain.
Although we are imperfect, and live in an imperfect world,
may we continue to love!

Palms Together,
Haemin Sunim

Haemin Sunim is one of the most influential Zen Buddhist teachers and writers in the world. Born in South Korea and educated at Berkeley, Harvard and Princeton, he received formal monastic training in Korea and taught Buddhism at Hampshire College in Massachusetts. He has more than a million followers on Twitter (@haeminsunim) and Facebook, and he lives in Seoul when not travelling to share his teachings.

Deborah Smith (translation) is the translator of Han Kang's *The Vegetarian*, which won the Man Booker International Prize in 2016.

Lisk Feng (illustrations) is an award-winning illustrator whose work has appeared in such publications as the *New Yorker*, *The New York Times*, the *Washington Post*, the *Wall Street Journal*, the *Los Angeles Times*, *Monocle* and *Travel + Leisure*.